Breakthrough MORE

7 Strategies to Help You Unlock Your Greatest Potential

Breakthrough MORE

*7 Strategies to Help You Unlock Your
Greatest Potential*

By Cory J. Chapman

Foreword by Les Brown

Success 4 UR Life

Breakthrough MORE

ISBN: 978-0-578-41964-0

Published by Success4urlife, Inc.

www.corychapman.com

What People Are Saying About *Breakthrough*:

"Only someone who's fought back, who's learned what it takes to not only come back but summit your challenges with heart and gusto and purpose can write a book like *Breakthrough*. These strategies define the core of a man I respect, trust, admire for his courage and his intuitive intelligence about life and business. These *Breakthrough* strategies are just that – your keys to living into your greater possibility. Make a promise to yourself to read *Breakthrough* today, and begin putting Cory's pragmatic wisdom into action starting tomorrow. Live your promise, leave all regrets behind, *Breakthrough*."
- Gary W. Goldstein, Speaker, Author and Hollywood Executive Producer

"This book will strengthen, enhance and change many lives! It will truly enable people to take themselves to the Next Level both personally and professional. My friend and colleague Cory Chapman has put it all on the line. Becoming transparent and vulnerable. This is the opportunity for the readers to hear from someone who has been up, down and up again. The important thing is that ups and downs are part of being alive and that now that he had developed and lived both the journey and the methods he can be assured that come what may, he will not survive but rather thrive!"
- Bob Donnell, Founder, Everything Next Level

"*Breakthrough* is a powerful reminder for every entrepreneur, founder and CEO that anything's possible when you push past your comfort zone. Whatever limits you from achieving your dreams, taking action with the simple strategies in this book will speed you to bigger results."
- Tommy Carr, CEO of Winners Winn, Inc., Author, Speaker

"Today's business climate is difficult and ever changing. It requires people to work longer and harder hours, sacrifice more personal time, and develop additional skills, just to maintain where you are, let alone get ahead. Cory Chapman's new book *Breakthrough* could be the potential game changer you may be searching for. Rather than just work harder, *Breakthrough* what you've always done to achieve what you never thought you could."
- Eski Felton, Entrepreneur and Fire Captain

"As a realtor for over 22 years, sometimes in life you just get stuck. I was fortunate to read *Breakthrough*, and in a short period of time I had a plan to get me back on track in Real Estate and help me find a new passion in the direct sales industry. This book will open your mind to new opportunities."
- Christy Lopez, Realtor and Professional Networker

"*Breakthrough* delivers a powerful reminder that anything's possible when you take action to push past your fears, and serves up simple, smart strategies to obliterate whatever limits have kept you from achieving your dreams."
- Steven Jones, CEO of The Solution Center, Coach and Speaker

"There's a big difference between being alive and truly living. I've felt both and the distance between the two is paved with tiny decisions. Your seemingly insignificant decision to pick up Cory Chapman's book *Breakthrough* can lead to a ripple effect that can completely change the path of your life. Cory is laying his heart on the line by sharing his own struggles and the principles that lead to his own *Breakthrough*! I challenge you don't just read this book, master it and start living again."
- Natalie Kilbourne, Entrepreneur and Professional Networker

"For over 10 years motivational speaking, training, and helping people build businesses have been my full-time profession. The principals in [Breakthrough], by Cory Chapman, are essential for any person wanting to get ahead in life or have a massive break-though. Cory has the unique ability helping individuals identify their strengths and weaknesses while offering superb wisdom and training - of which can be found in this book. Give heed to his advice, follow his advice and your break-through will happen."
- Jared Overton, Founder of Wake Up and Change, Entrepreneur

"Cory Chapman not only lives these steps towards Breakthrough, but coaches others to do the same. Having been on the receiving end of his wisdom he presses for your truth. This book helps you look in the mirror and outlines those steps for you to do some deep, personal reflection, to propel you towards your goals. Don't wither on the vine, read and grow with this book."
- Nadine Rothermel, Director, Leadership Development Programs

Dedication to My Wife

This book is dedicated to my best friend, soul mate and the mother of my children, my beautiful wife, Delilah. When I think of all you have had to endure being the wife of an entrepreneur, but not just any entrepreneur: me! This is a whole other level, (smile).

I wanted to take this time to publicly explain how much you mean to me. There is not a day that goes by that you don't make me better. You are my strength when I'm having a hard day, my conscious when I'm having bad thoughts and my inspiration to continue moving forward toward success. The day God brought you into my life was the day He sent an angel to save me. I don't know where I would be today without you. You have given me three amazing and wonderful children, who continue to WOW me every day. You make me better.

I Love You,

Your Babe!

Table of Contents

Foreword by Les Brown

As we look at the world today, with all of its uncertainty and tremendous change, the question is: *What does it take to make it today?* Thirty years ago, people were looking for one thing… a "break." You know what I mean, an opportunity, a green light, a "foot in the door" that would open up new possibilities. Presently, people need more than a simple "break," "scratch" or "crack" onto the surface of potential, they need a Breakthrough!

A Breakthrough is not just a mere opportunity; it is a mindset that unleashes limitless opportunities! Many people go through life mistaking, or "miss-taking," their mistakes. They "miss" what they needed to "take" from difficulty in order to gain in life. Most people don't need a chance, they need a change in mindset; they need a Breakthrough!

This book was designed to help you discover a part of yourself that you haven't met yet. There is a you that you long to be but have yet to become. In Breakthrough, Cory provides a roadmap for you to Breakthrough the barriers that hinder you from achieving higher dimensions of greatness in your life.

Ask yourself, "What steps will it take for me to get ahead in life?"

Take the first step: Commitment. Commitment is the willingness to be all in and give your best at all times. Regardless of the circumstances, be willing to commit. Commit because it's who are! Secondly, be Optimistic. The primary difference between the optimist and the cynic is a cynic can't see opportunities because they are too busy being blinded by obstacles! An optimist, on the other-hand overcomes obstacles and seizes opportunities. Thirdly, consider your **R**elationship capital. You must develop a community of collaborative, achievement-driven relationships that give you a competitive advantage.

Your company will accompany you along the path that you choose for yourself. Choose your company with your "final destination" in mind! Be selective, it's critical in order to reach your desired outcome. In each of us, there is a yearning for more.

The final step is to Yield. **Y**ield to the yearning! Don't just "yearn" and stop. Yield to the passion that is in your heart. Surrender! After all, you have greatness within you! Cory Chapman, a dynamic speaker, trainer and gifted author has created a body of work that will guide you through a step-by-step process to allow you to live your greatest life.

I have had the pleasure of being in the audience as he mesmerizes with his presence, charisma, and most of all, his knowledge of what it takes to "Breakthrough." He will show you how to "get unstuck" and move freely through your fears, doubts, and circumstances that seek to hold you captive. Each chapter of this book will give you a better vision of yourself beyond circumstances and negative mental conditioning.

Cory is my spiritual son and I am very proud of him. He is the message that he brings. Undoubtedly, he is destined to change the world. He has overcome tremendous challenges and exemplifies the fact that your past doesn't have to be your present or determine your future. At any moment, you can decide that enough is enough. You can choose a better path for yourself; one that is more fulfilling and true to who you really are. This book will serve as a blueprint and guide to empower you to navigate through the storms of life as you soar to new heights.

Get ready for your Breakthrough!

- Les Brown, Speaker/Speaker Coach/Author

Introduction:
I Don't Need a Break – I Need a Breakthrough!

"Fall seven times, stand up eight."
- Japanese Proverb

It was 4:30 in the morning. I woke up out of a sound sleep. I was suddenly and undeniably wide awake. It might as well have been noon for how suddenly and energetically awake I was; and not in a good way. My pulse was pounding; my heart, too.

Suddenly, and without warning, I decided I was going to get a JOB.

You see, I had been self-employed for years and had always been able to make a living. In fact, we had a very good lifestyle. Nice cars, a beautiful home, all the "toys" a family could ever want, plus we traveled frequently with our amazing kids. We had had a good run, but like everything else in life, things had changed.

The career – and industry – that had served me so well, for so long, had changed. The clients that used to knock down my door weren't so easy to come by anymore and, even when they did appear, our overhead was so high, I had to get more and more of them just to keep up with where we were, let alone get ahead. I could see the future getting tighter and tighter, and the thought of working that much harder just to stay in place made my heart pound even faster.

1

Each passing month was like a roller coaster ride, with plenty of ups and downs, emotional highs and lows – and everything in between. There was little to no stability and I found myself obsessing over where the next cash infusion might come from, if it came at all.

Our income level was inconsistent, with ups and downs and highs and lows, which resulted in us being late on our bills more than once. With the economy in decline and no new clients knocking at my door, I'd been knocked down; flat. And this time, for the first time, I couldn't get up from the canvas after the ten count.

It wasn't just the lack of clients or even the mounting bills. In the past, I'd always been able to bounce back when times got tough, or even hustle up some side job to make ends meet. But not this time. I seemed unable to put anything together. Calling in my markers hadn't worked and nothing new was on the horizon. My confidence was shaken, my swag was gone, and I was starting to panic.

As wide awake as if it were noon, I got out of bed and went to my home office, not wanting to alert the rest of the family about my mounting concerns. I paced the darkened room over and over again, heart pounding with anxiety as I tried to both understand and do damage control around my – around our – situation.

My mind raced as question after question required my attention:

- How are we going to pay our bills?
- What will we use to buy the groceries?
- What am I going to do to cover the house note next month?

2

- What if there's an emergency and the car needs a new transmission?
- What if one of us gets sick and we have to go to the doctor?
- What if the kids need to go to the dentist?
- How will I pay the tuition for our daughter's school on Monday?

Worst, of all, the IRS was also closing in and we had to figure out how we were going to pay our back taxes, which included thousands of dollars we obviously didn't have. We had previously filed bankruptcy, so this was no longer an option.

I needed a break, a brainstorm, a flash of light, an inspiration or a jackpot or some kind of jolt to jumpstart my career, my life, get my confidence, mojo and swagger back.

I knew if I could just find the right gear, I could really let loose and gain back all the ground I'd lost, then go even farther. But I was stuck in neutral, grinding my gears, spinning my wheels. Why couldn't I come up with anything? Why was it so much harder to get revitalized this time than ever before?

Somehow, I knew, I needed *more* than just a "break". That wasn't going to be enough for me this time. A temporary fix, a quick loan or cash infusion just wouldn't do the trick. I needed a Breakthrough. A game changing, level leaping, do-over, start from scratch, hit the "restart" button Breakthrough to kick me out of neutral, rev up my engine and put me back on the fast track to success.

Not a Break, But a Breakthrough!

The late great Jim Rohn once said something that always stuck with me, "Don't wish the problem would be smaller; ask for more skills to solve your problems." That's what I needed; not a quick fix, but a life changing, habit forming solution. Not a break, but a Breakthrough! In other words, I didn't need to solve my current problems. I had to learn a way to be better, faster, stronger and smarter to avoid them the next time.

So how to be better? FAST! I mean, I needed something with the quickness or our financial situation was going to go from bad to worse. Well, when your back is up against a wall and you've got nowhere to turn, you can either lay down and die or you can come out fighting.

I chose the latter. And, if you're reading a book called *Breakthrough*, it's obvious that you have, too. And that's good, because this book is all about breaking through what you've always done to achieve what you never thought you could.

My 7 Strategies to Help You Unlock Your Greatest Potential

How? How do you go from just "getting a break" to achieving a Breakthrough? Well, you can achieve this feat by using my **7 Strategies to Help You Unlock Your Greatest Potential:**

1. **Where Are You?** Before you can chart a path for where you want to go – or even before deciding where you want to go – it is critical that you already know where you are. Thus, the first strategy is simply to ask, "Where am I?" Once you answer that question, you can move onto the next strategy, which is:

2. **What's Holding You Back?** Oftentimes we live our entire lives without ever once stopping to consider why we're not quite where we thought we would be. Knowing what's holding you back isn't a solution in itself, but questioning the traits, habits, defeating self-talk and other influences or factors that are keeping you from success is a vital strategy in learning to Breakthrough.

3. **Reduce The Noise:** Our lives are filled with clutter, most of it self-created. We surround ourselves with distractions – which I call "noise" – that are both internal and external in nature. Some distractions are easier to reduce than others, while many prove more challenging. Breakthroughs require constant concentration, concerted effort and excellence, so until you learn to reduce the noise, you can't achieve your ultimate goal because you will always be less than totally focused on the task at hand.

4. **Dream Big:** It's not a Breakthrough if you can get there in an hour! You must dream big. This strategy will help you go farther, try harder, dig deeper and dream bigger to ensure that you aren't just doing your best, but pushing yourself to make your best even better!

5. **Strengthen Your Why:** Do you know "why" you do the things you do? Struggle against the grain? Try to be your best? Or hang out with the people you do? Why go to so much trouble? Why not just settle for mediocrity and ignore the big Breakthrough this book will help you achieve? Until you know "why" you want a better life, you will find it more and more difficult to achieve. This strategy will help you answer your "why" to get to your "what's next".

6. **Become A Better You:** Life is not a straight line with "start" marked at one end and "finish" at the other. It is a journey, marked by twists and turns that never quite ends until we do. The goal of this strategy is to form a lifelong, habitual commitment to becoming a smarter, wiser, better you. Never stop improving, and you'll never stop succeeding.

7. **All Out Massive Action (A.O.M.A.)** Our last strategy provides the fuse that will ignite the entire powder keg that is your full potential. Dreaming, thinking, planning, even knowing isn't enough to Breakthrough. You need to take the six previous strategies and apply a heaping helping of All Out Massive Action, or A.O.M.A., to give your dreams marching orders!

One by one, these seven simple strategies will improve your chances for success and take you to that next level you need to Breakthrough and reach goals you never thought possible before. Each strategy is a success booster on its own but, collectively, all seven strategies will truly **Help You Unlock Your Greatest Potential.**

The Takeaway

But first, I think it's necessary to "warm up" with a little pre-strategy session as I share with you how I arrived at these seven strategies and ultimately used them to achieve my own Breakthrough.

Also, at the end of each chapter – yes, even the Introduction – I've included a series of Action Steps, in the form of probing questions or guiding thoughts, that I'd like you to answer before moving to the next chapter:

Action Steps for the Introduction

Questions are never wasted, and I believe searching for the answers is one of the best ways we can better ourselves each and every day. Before you get started putting the lessons I've shared in this Introduction, ask yourself these simple questions:

Have I ever had a Breakthrough before?

If so, what did it look like?

Which of the seven strategies seems most compelling to me?

Which seems the most intimidating?

Do I have the time and energy to commit to my Breakthrough, starting today?!?

Chapter 1:
The Pre-Strategy – What's My Story?

"By altering our attitudes we can alter our lives"
- Zig Ziglar

Why should you listen to me? What do I have to say and why am I the right one to say it? Great question! (Or should I say, great questions!) You've probably never heard of me before and, even if you had, I'd still be a complete stranger. So why? Why listen to someone else about how to change your own circumstance?

The fact is, I've learned as much from my failures as I have from my successes and, if you read my story and heed my advice, you can not only learn from the mistakes I made – but how to avoid them. You can also learn the strategies and insights I implemented to help you on your journey to success, as well as to help you avoid life's most common pitfalls along the way.

I don't know many people would have – or even *could* have – survived in the entrepreneurial world as I did. I reached incredible heights, tumbled to unthinkable lows, then succeeded – and failed – all over again! If you can learn from my journey, and the things that I share can make you a better person and give you the strength to Breakthrough from what's holding you back, then it was all worth it!

"What" was all worth it? What have I endured and how can my story help inform, change, write or even rewrite your story? Read on to find out:

Humble Beginnings; Bright Future

I was born in Brooklyn, New York and raised by a single mom. I have two brothers that live in different parts of the country. I always felt that my mom was a "ROCK" because she single-handedly raised three African-American boys in two major cities, and none of them were in a gang, did drugs, had children out of wedlock or ended up in jail.

We had a good life. My mom worked several jobs to make enough money to keep a roof over our heads and food on the table. Despite working all hours of the day and night, she always provided for us and made sure that we never wanted for anything, even if it was just a little advice or quiet conversation when I know she must have been exhausted. But like the ROCKSTAR she was, she always lent an ear – or a pearl of wisdom – depending on the situation.

As a single mom it was hard on her, and on us, but Mom always made a way. Life couldn't have been easy for her, personally speaking, but she stayed positive and tried to instill strong family values in her children – and she did.

As for a dad, I never knew my biological father. From what I was told he was a very mean drunk who was extremely abusive to my mother. In fact, it wasn't until he tried to hurt me that my mother found the strength to leave him once and for all, and do it on her own!

To this day I'm a firm believer that there is something to be said about a mother's love for her child, and I'm not sure where I or my siblings might be if mom hadn't worked so hard to keep a roof over our head, love in our home, wisdom between our ears and strength in our hearts. Somehow, someway, we always survived.

After high school I joined the Navy as a way to serve my country and afford a brighter future for myself through education. I had always been intrigued by the law so, upon leaving the military, I thought I would become a lawyer. Now that I think about it, I wasn't so much intrigued with the law itself as I was with the *money* that I knew lawyers could make. But at least I had a goal.

A Cold Dose of Reality

After my humble beginnings and watching my mother raise her kids while working two and sometimes three jobs and then going through the military myself, I was tired of being broke and just barely scraping by. I was tired of merely "making enough" just to get along, with no extras, perks or fringe benefits on the side. Now that I was on my own, I wanted more from my life. I wanted to be successful, with all the bells and whistles that ensured: big house, nice cars, exotic vacations, nice bank account, spending money, expensive toys and everything in between.

On TV lawyers always looked really successful, so I thought I would give it a try. After all, what did I have to lose? So I started attending school to become a paralegal, the idea being that once I was established and making a living, I would then apply to law school and make it "official". Or, so I thought! True to my hustling spirit, before I even graduated I started working for a huge law firm as a paralegal while still going to school to *become* a paralegal.

They were paying me $15.00 an hour and, at the time, I thought I was in heaven. Once the dust settled and I started working for them, however, I realized that what I thought I wanted wasn't what I was actually getting. Not even close. I was getting there early, staying late and working on Saturdays and Sundays just to make the partners look good, and they were billing my time out at $40.00 an hour, of which I was only getting $15.00 an hour. That meant they were making nearly twice as much as I was for doing absolutely nothing. It was the best scam I'd ever seen; I did all the work and, in exchange for chump change, they made $25 in pure profit for every hour of my hard labor.

But that wasn't the worst of it. I watched clients basically get ripped off from the very people that were supposed to be helping them in their times of need. Needless to say, I had to make a change. The sooner, the better.

So instead of racing to work for someone else again, I started my own paralegal company where I started billing out *my* services out for $40.00 an hour! Not bad for a kid from the streets of Brooklyn that never finished college. I was 21 and living well for the first time in my life, but I knew there was more to the story than the glimpse I'd gotten with my first taste as an entrepreneur. In part of my ongoing education in all things entrepreneurial, I saw an article that immediately caught my eye: it said stockbrokers averaged $100,000 a year.

So I thought to myself, "I should do that." And I did: by the end of the summer I had found a company that was willing to train me as an insurance and securities broker and put me on the path to more wealth. My first year in the business I broke every record at my new company; I was both the newest and the *top* life insurance salesperson in the office. At the time, I was also the youngest – and the only – African-American male in the office. I made $187,000 my first full year in the game. Yes!

Some Things Aren't Always What They Seem

I had arrived, not just a little – but by a lot. With both my Securities License *and* my Insurance License in hand, the sky was literally the limit. Or, again, so I thought! Little did I know it, but I was in for another nasty surprise in the world of business. The managing partner of the company I worked for had already started grooming me to take over the office one day.

By my third year I was the assistant managing director and still crushing production. By year five, my mentor – who was also the managing director at the company – was ready to retire and have me take over the company for him. This was it; my first executive level role in a major company, and I wasn't even thirty yet.

The only problem was that it had to be approved by the home office. Now, I knew this was just a formality because I had out produced, worked harder and gave more of myself than anyone else at the office – by a mile. There was no one else even close. I was already handling the day to day activities of the office, basically, and most of the staff looked to me for leadership. As far as I was concerned, this was a done deal.

Still, there were hoops to jump through and protocol to follow. For starters, the home office wanted to meet in person and talk to me "face to face," so we flew out to corporate to have an official "meet and greet." I was on Cloud 9, never expecting that, in the course of one 24-hour day, I'd be firmly back on planet earth nursing a crushed ego.

The whole trip there, I knew this was a lock; so did everyone back home. No one doubted I was the right man for the job, including my boss and early mentor who, after all, had handpicked me to replace him! But when I walked in the room that morning I was in for the shock of my young life. I had never seen more people so surprised to see me and, for the first time in my life, I understood what racism – cold, hard racism – was.

The looks on the faces of those men and women in that boardroom gave me one of the most uncomfortable feelings I had ever felt. You could have cut the tension in that room with a knife and after just a little time spent there, I got the feeling that nothing I could say would change the minds of these bigoted individuals.

By the time we returned back to the office on Friday, we had gotten word from corporate that I wasn't "seasoned" enough to run this shop and that I should give it "a few more years" before I was ready. "But," the corporate office added, "please help us with a smooth transition with your new boss so he can get up to speed." Needless to say, I was not happy.

My mentor thought it was wrong, people in the office thought it was wrong, but there it was, just the same; the decision had been made – and it wasn't in my favor. What was I supposed to do?

Well, me being me, I promptly started planning my exit that very weekend. I contacted my largest clients, told them I was thinking about opening my own firm and that I would like them to come with me. By the end of that weekend I had managed to get commitments from more than 80% of my largest clients, which was more than enough to hang my own shingle and strike out on my own. By the end of the following week I had obtained a broker-dealer relationship and resigned from my former company to start my own firm, called The IMOC Group.

Founder and CEO

The IMOC Group started off strong and only went uphill from there. From day one, it all just clicked. I was happy, my new staff was happy, the clients were happy and, just as importantly – maybe even more importantly, for some – we were all making money. Things were going extremely well and, before I knew it, we had completed our fifth year in business breaking all projections – and new ground – nearly every one of those years.

It was the kind of success one can only dream of but, while it's happening, you tend to take it for granted. Having hustled my whole career, having out-produced, out maneuvered and out-flanked everyone from my competition to my former employer(s), I figured this was how it was supposed to be – and how it would always be.

I mean, what could go wrong?

In the course of those five years we had built a 5,000-square-foot office space that cost a little over $300,000. It was top-notch craftsmanship, state of the art technology and all the creature comforts – for ourselves and our clients – rolled into one.

With the kind of profits we were seeing, I was able to hire amazing staff and recruit talent from all over the country. My clients were the cream of the crop, and so was the staff I hired to service them. No expense was spared, and it paid off in increasingly diverse and wealthy clientele. I even started thinking about expanding into becoming our own Broker Dealer and Investment advisory firm.

For the first time ever, our revenue was over a million dollars and I had made a high six-figure income that I actually got to see in my accounts. It wasn't just on paper, promised, projected or in "stock options". No, it was cold, hard, cash, operating capital for my own personal fortune, money I could instantly see, count and use at my discretion.

I was finally living the American Dream: I was under 30, wildly successful, goal-oriented, established and wealthy. The next steps were to become bigger in our industry, establish a foothold on the competition and market a distinctive, unique, targeted brand to attract more – and more affluent – clients.

The best way to do that was by becoming a broker dealer. A college friend of mine suggested that, instead of creating my own brokerage-dealer firm, why not avoid all the headaches of startup with the paperwork and investments and merge with an existing broker dealer instead? I thought that sounded like pretty good advice.

This way I could get the company up and running more quickly and, by merging with someone already established, not only piggyback on their infrastructure but learn from their wisdom as well. After searching for the right fit, we ultimately joined forces with MAS Capital Securities, Inc.

Rather than a pure partnership, 50-50, my company would be consumed by MAS instead. Accordingly, I would become the Chief Operating Officer (COO) and Vice President (VP) of MAS. Once I transferred my assets to MAS, everything would be complete and we could start bringing in bigger deals.

I settled in and worked hard, as usual, watching the market with a closer appreciation and learning everything I could about my new business venture in order to master it in as little time as possible, as I had the other previous entities I'd been involved with.

You've heard the phrase "from good to great?" Apparently, there's a flip side to that trend and, as the months went on, I learned the flip side firsthand. That's because things went from "great" to just "good" to flat-out "monumentally, disastrously bad" – and fast.

Turns out the partnership – and our timing – couldn't have been worse. The Dot.Com bubble of 2000-2002 had resulted in over 5 trillion dollars in lost earnings for the stock market. My new business partner – and owner of MAS Capital – had never been a trader or been involved with correction in the markets, and thus was suddenly out of his league.

"While You Were Out..."

As the losses from the Dot.Com burst started mounting and the news grew more and more grim, my business partner and majority shareholder started to panic, particularly when our revenues finally began going in the opposite direction. While I was out of town for my wife's birthday, he decided to cut his losses and shut down our business – without consulting me first.

While I was away from the office he fired all of our staff, closed the doors and canceled all the phone lines. Mind you, this was during the worst period in the stock market since the Great Depression. During the worst trading week ever, many of the clients I had worked so hard for all those years were trying to get in touch with me but, with the phones turned off, were unable to.

One of my staff members finally got in touch with me while we were out of town but, by the time we got back, the office was locked up tight and, to make matters worse, the locks had been changed by the landlord of the building. Because the lease was in the new company's name, which I no longer had any authorization to use, they would not allow us back into the office.

The same office I had built from scratch.

I felt sick, confused, betrayed, anxious and, ultimately, defeated. I had always worked hard to be ethical and trustworthy in my business dealings and, naively I suppose, had assumed others would act the same. Apparently not.

My so called "partner" had disappeared with the company's assets, all of them, and, financially speaking, I was done. The clients that I had managed for years were frustrated and scared and, naturally, decided to look for other brokers to manage their money. Or, at least, what was left of it after the dust cleared on the stock market floor.

My assets were all in the name of MAS Capital, so I had to fight through arbitration to get them back, which would take time; time I didn't have. My physical office was no longer accessible to us, along with files and computers. For all intents and purposes, everything I built for the last six years was gone!

All the hard work, all the effort, all the late nights and missed meals and birthdays and holidays and weekends, just when everything was going so well, it was wiped away with a single decision. Not even my own decision.

It seemed inconceivable to me that a split-second decision made by one person could radically alter the fates of so many others, without even being given the option of weighing in on the matter. It wasn't just me who'd lost everything. Many of the staff I'd personally hired and trained during those six years went down with the ship as well. They may not have had as much invested in the company as I did, but they lost things just as valuable as money: momentum, time, confidence and, worst of all, trust.

That was what hurt the most, I think: the betrayal of trust. Maybe it was because it was my first time being betrayed, but the betrayal cut deep, and left me wiped out – and ticked off.

I had been raised by a single mother who worked every day of her life pursuing the American dream, and who taught her children to pursue it as well. We grew up believing that we could be anything we wanted to be, that the only limitations on our success were our own dreams. But I forgot that others could rob you of your entire future, all without holding a gun!

After fighting depression and the courts and everything else that had been going on during this time, I finally got back on my feet. With the grace of God and the strength of my beautiful wife, Delilah, I finally got my butt back into the game.

I remember reading a book about Donald Trump and it talked about how he lost billions over the course of his lifetime, and yet he was still able to recover from it. I figured if he could suffer that kind of loss and come out on top, I could certainly triumph over my current situation, bleak as it may have seemed at the time.

I remember a quote from the book that said, "No matter how much I lost, I could rebuild it again because they hadn't taken my knowledge from me." That stuck with me because Trump was so right. Knowledge is the one thing we – and we alone – possess and no one can take it from us. After realizing that, I was determined to win at all costs, no matter how much had been taken from me. I still had my knowledge, I still had the skills and drive and talent and know-how to do it all over again, and that's exactly what I began to do.

I started reaching out to friends and old clients, trying to get my business – or *some* business – back up and running again. Soon enough, a few of my friends decided to go into business with me. But this time it would be different. Instead of a dictatorship, where one signature could decide the fate of the entire company without requiring the consideration, let alone the permission, of the rest of the organization, this new entity would be a group of partners and we would each have a say in the structure of our business.

Nor would we ever have just one revenue stream coming in, making us vulnerable if, as had happened when the Dot.Com bubble burst, it dried up. Instead, we would diversify. We would grow in many sectors, like real estate, mortgage lending and securities. This company would be the best of the best, an elite group of entrepreneurs dedicated to achieving only excellence for their clients. Appropriately enough, we would call it Elite Financial Center, Inc.

New Beginnings, New Problems

In September of 2003 we formed the company and started working our way back to the top of the game. Through hard work and determination, by August of 2006 – less than three years of being in business – we had surpassed the revenue I was making from my previous company.

They say that the best revenge is living well, and surpassing my previous success even after being completely wiped out by it proved those words to be absolutely true. Living well meant that I could forget, if not entirely forgive, my old business partner for his betrayal, and focus on the task at hand, which turned out to be dominating the local investment scene.

It was the height of the real estate market in California; we were making money on purchases, sales and lending. Not to mention our securities arm was growing as well. The stock market was up, interest rates were down and business was thriving.

We had enough money to build out a premier financial center in Culver City, California. We hired a full staff and recruited fifteen loan officers, six real estate agents and even a couple of securities representatives to ensure the office was well-rounded and completely prepared for any serious client who walked through the door. We had a business model that was attractive to agents and brokers in the securities and lending industry, to whit:

- **Get multiple licenses so that you can advise your clients on multiple transactions.**
- **Leave nothing on the table.**
- **Make sure you can help your clients maximize their net worth by having the expertise to advise them in all key areas of their wealth buckets.**
- **Be absolutely, 200% committed to providing experience, expertise and excellence during every transaction, for every client.**

We continued to grow and build and, most importantly, make money. At the height of this business we were spending approximately $32,000 a month in overhead and salaries. Sounds pricey, but not when you consider the fact that, on average, we were bringing in $50,000 to $70,000 **a month**. As a direct lender, we had a warehouse line of credit of over 10 million dollars. We had lines of credit of $500,000 and we had credit cards that had $50,000 credit limits.

Life was better than it had ever been. (Or so I thought!) Well, like I said earlier on in this chapter, everything always changes and, if it doesn't, you're probably doing something wrong. It was September of 2008, and the subprime market had just collapsed. Unfortunately, at the time, we had several millions of dollars worth of mortgages waiting to get sold on the open market. We were on the hook for it!

As the day went on, and I can recall it vividly even now, the stock market started to react to the subprime market and we started seeing record lows. Now, mind you, I had been here before and the markets had always corrected. In my mind, rather than panic and cut our losses, we just needed to weather the storm, wait it out and hold strong.

"This will pass," I told everyone who would listen, including myself. "Just stay in the game and we'll make it through."

Through my confidence and belief, I was able to talk everyone down for the time being. But as the week progressed, things were getting scarier and more troubling. Even I was starting to doubt my own advice! We couldn't sell the loans that we had outstanding in the secondary market, and were on the hook for a six-figure amount if they didn't get sold.

The lines of credit were being rejected by the banks and now we were getting margin calls on our company portfolio. Suddenly, the partners were starting to waver and wanted to jump ship. Still, despite the market conditions and warning signs, I was determined not to lose this one again. I knew if we gave in, all of our staff would be without jobs and, more personally, I would be without a business once more.

How could this be happening? I wondered in my darkest, most private moments. It seemed inconceivable that after weathering the Dot.Com bubble and burst, losing it all and rebuilding everything better than before, I was about to repeat this process of losing everything all over again.

I had learned so much from my previous upset, and thought I had protected myself, insulated myself, from this kind of "perfect storm" again. For once, I thought I had conceived of a business model that would be virtually untouchable. After all, we were in three different sectors, spreading the risk around: real estate, mortgage lending and financial planning.

No way that all of these sectors could go down at the same time, I thought, but sure enough: they did. As the partners got more and more frightened, they wanted to throw in the towel and bankrupt the warehouse line. Personally, I still wanted to ride it out, thinking – hoping – this was just a correction in the market and that it would eventually recover.

I mean, even if we had to take significant losses right up until the last minute, I would still rather be in business at the end of the day than take ourselves out of the game without trying everything possible to correct ourselves. While my wife and I were determined not to lose this business, ultimately, the partners decided to bail out. In their absence, we decided to pay for the warehouse line and hold on to the office ourselves.

It was a risky gamble, to be sure: if everything would settle out the way we hoped it would, the markets leveled out and returned to normal, we would come out on top and, what's more, be free of our partners to reap all the benefits ourselves. We would own the company outright, and enjoy a tremendous payday once the loans were sold.

What's more, our staff would get to keep their jobs and the doors would stay open, signifying trust, competence and confidence to current and potential clients. But if we were wrong, it would wipe us out all over again. It seemed inconceivable that we could face such hardship twice in a lifetime, let alone a single decade, and so my wife and I spun the wheel, bought the ticket and took the ride until the very end. Well, sure enough, thirty-five days later the economy had the worst downturn in over thirty years.

The subprime market collapsed and, suddenly, no bank would touch those kinds of loans with a ten foot pole. The real estate market values in California dropped by 30% in less than three months, and the stock market lost almost 40% in one month alone.

I gambled and lost once again. Overnight, or so it seemed, the business was upside down and the overhead was sucking us dry while revenue had halted to a complete stop. Now, I'm sure by now you're saying to yourself, "Dang, can he get a break?! This is something straight out of a movie."

Well, it happened, and I'm living proof that you can survive that kind of life lesson and still survive, even thrive. But enough about me. Now it's time to talk about you:

So, What's Your Story?

Now that I've shared my story, I want you to stop for a moment and ask yourself:

- *What's my story?*
- *Where am I, right now, that I find myself reading a book called Breakthrough?*
- *What brought me here and where am I headed next?*

It's that "next" part I want to talk to you about, because that's where we're headed. Where I've been, that's behind me. I'll never forget it, it informs my every waking moment and, in fact, as you'll find out later, provided my "why" for my biggest Breakthrough yet. But I can't go back and change the past; only learn from it and keep moving forward.

I would say the same to you. It is important to study your story from a historical perspective, because where you've been often has a significant impact on where you're going. But nothing in your past dictates your future like how you feel in the present. By that I mean, focus on today, not tomorrow. How you feel about yourself today may be an echo of yesterday, but don't let it keep writing your script day after day after day.

We have a tendency to hang onto past experiences like so much baggage, cluttering up our lives and weighing us down. While every experience adds to who we are in the present, if we dwell too much on the past we simply can't enjoy the present, let alone anticipate or plan for the future.

So tell your story, examine it, know it well, but use it to propel you forward, not hold you back. Before we begin our journey together, I invite you to pause in your reading and envision how you might tell your story much as I told mine.

Say it out loud, write it down, or simply reflect quietly on the life experiences, journey and developments that have brought you to this place in time.

Ask yourself:

- *Who have been the major players in my life?*
- *Who have been my biggest influencers?*
- *What have they taught me?*
- *What did I teach them?*

- *What would I characterize as my life's four or five biggest teaching moments?*
- *What did I learn from them?*
- *How did they affect me?*
- *If my life was a book, what would I call it?*
- *Who would read it?*
- *Who should read it, and why?*

These questions, and this exercise, should help put you in the proper state of mind before determining your future. We all want to get wherever we're going as quickly as possible, and in fact part of the Breakthrough process is the element of speed. But it never hurts to push the "pause" button and reflect, particularly if you turn the activity into an exercise that helps you prepare for what's next.

The Takeaway

Moving forward, my goal with this book is to teach you how to Breakthrough. After hearing my story, you might be thinking to yourself, "Hey, compared to this guy, my story isn't so bad after all. Why am I here? Remind me why I'm reading this again? What am I going to learn from all of this?"

Well, I'm going to teach you how to learn from the past, embrace the present, fail forward and, finally, Breakthrough. How? Using my **7 Strategies to Help You Unlock Your Greatest Potential**, I'm going to show you what's holding you back and how to move forward to achieve things you never imagined.

On the following pages you will read more about each of my seven strategies, understand its "link" in the chain of your own success and how they all fit together to create an unbeatable, unstoppable, unlimited new you!

So get ready, your journey to a fabulous new Breakthrough starts on the very next page:

Action Steps for Chapter 1

Before you get started using the lessons I've shared in Chapter 1, ask yourself these simple questions:

Have I owned my own story and am I ready to use it to prepare me for the future?

Looking back, what is the biggest lesson my life story taught me about who I really am?

If I could write a new life story, what would it say?

What do I know about myself after reading this chapter than I didn't know before?

What do I know about the 7 Strategies to Help You Unlock Your Greatest Potential that I didn't know before?

Chapter 2:
The First Strategy – Where Are You?

"I have not failed. I've just found 10,000 ways that won't work."
- Thomas A. Edison

Though my story definitely had its ups and downs, disappointments and outright failures, looking back on it now… it doesn't seem quite so bad. Perhaps that's because I'm on the other side now, recovering, surviving… heading in the right direction toward a much brighter future than ever before.

Maybe it's because I've lived through all that and realized that there is life after failure – even life after *multiple* failures. Perhaps I've learned not to "sweat the small stuff," and to focus on the bigger picture versus the minute details. Or maybe it's because I now know the true value of those life experiences and how I couldn't be on a clearer path to success right now if it weren't for those setbacks, roadblocks and challenges in my rearview mirror.

You might even say that those ups and downs, setbacks and failures made me the success I am today. That I am, after all, the sum of my parts and that, without those hard times, I couldn't be enjoying the good times I am right now.

Rare is the success story without the failure story. The difference is, we don't tend to brag on what we've lost, only on what we've gained. Donald Trump isn't shy about admitting the millions, even billions, he's lost over the years, but he'd much rather show you his latest high rise success story as a testament to his self-worth.

Everyone likes to think that Walt Disney had the Midas touch, that everything he touched turn to magical castles, Hollywood blockbusters or theme park platinum. But like I said, few success stories are written without a few failures in the footnotes.

And, in fact, Walt Disney once said this about the upside of failure, "I think it's important to have a good hard failure when you're young. I learned a lot out of that. Because it makes you kind of aware of what can happen to you. Because of it I've never had any fear in my whole life when we've been near collapse and all of that. I've never been afraid. I've never had the feeling I couldn't walk out and get a job doing something."

Young or old, rich or poor, who of us hasn't had a "good, hard failure" along the way? The only thing that keeps those crises failures is if you don't take them and turn them into learning experiences, never to repeat them again.

Like I always say, "You can't have a 'testimony' without first going through the test." What would life be without its heartbreaks and setbacks and life lessons and learning lessons? It would be nice to avoid all of life's unpleasantness, but I think we all understand that life just doesn't work out that way.

The Challenge: *Your Personal Q & A*

And honestly, what is life without challenge? How interesting would life be if we simply did the same thing, day after day, successfully and without interference from the hands of fate? Would we ever really learn if we never really failed?

Are we here simply to exist? To feel comfortable and safe and unchallenged? Or should our lives have purpose, forged in the fire of failure, defeat, trials and tribulations so that we come out on the other side, better prepared to meet life's challenges and even overcome them?

Based on my life experiences, and what they have meant to me, I have come up with a series of ten questions designed to test you, challenge you, excite you, revive you and, most of all, bring you closer to your very own Breakthrough. These ten questions are specifically designed to prepare you for the bulk of this chapter, which includes some more questions that I will not only answer myself, but help you answer as well.

For now, though, I want you to ask yourself the following ten questions to see where you are, right now, at this very moment. Every journey has a destination, but each has a starting point as well. Knowing both – your start and your finish line – will better prepare you for the journey ahead.

To get the most out of this exercise, be honest and remember, no one will ever know your answers unless you decide to discuss them with somebody else. (Which, come to think of it, isn't necessarily a bad idea!)

Sit somewhere calm, quiet and collected. Breathe, relax and open yourself to the moment. Give yourself plenty of time, as well. Exercises like these are too valuable to rush. Get comfortable where you are, body, mind and soul, and focus on the task at hand.

After each question, write a simple, one-word response to each of the following ten questions below:

1. Am I happy with my life? _____
2. Do I feel I have accomplished anything meaningful? _____
3. Does my life have purpose? _____
4. What am I passionate about? _____
5. Have I made a difference in someone else's life? _____
6. If I was to die today, would there be anyone at my funeral? _____
7. Have I accomplished what I set out to? _____
8. Does my current reality reflect how I really want to live? _____
9. Am I happy when I look in the mirror? _____
10. Am I holding myself back from greatness? _____

How did you do? Did you answer more "yes" questions than "no" questions? Did you answer the questions quickly, or did each take some thought? Were you on the fence about any of them, wondering if you gave the "right" answer?

Don't worry; there is no grade for this Q & A, no "right" or "wrong" answers, only an increased awareness of one's self and the ability to move forward with the knowledge that you're one step closer to knowing where you are in the present.

Why is this exercise so important? Can't we just get started on the strategies and get over all this self-exploration? Well, actually, to explore one's self is to know one's self, and to know one's self is to recognize our power. And if I know one thing, the more powerful you are, the more powerful your Breakthrough will be.

Too often we just drift through life, going nowhere but thinking we're moving forward when, after all, we're merely standing still. When we don't question why we do something, or even how we do something, we are doomed to repeat it over and over and over again.

Questioning ourselves helps us understand that we might not be as far along as we thought we were. Each question, and answer, shines a spotlight on an area of our life we either examine too rarely, or not at all. It may be uncomfortable to ask these questions, to ponder whether or not we're living the life we imagined we would, or even impacting the lives of others. In fact, some of these questions can really get to the heart of where we are in life and, if we're unsatisfied with the answers, where we need to go.

Have you ever gone on a diet? What was the first thing you did – weighed yourself, right? Well, this whole chapter is a lot like getting on the scale, only this scale doesn't measure how much you weigh, it measures how honest you are. These questions, guiding and open-ended, will help you discover where your "starting line" for success is.

You may be closer to a Breakthrough than you think, or farther away than you ever imagined. But if you never check the map – i.e. start to ask yourself questions about your current destination – how will you ever know?

And now that you've warmed yourself up and gotten to know yourself a little better, hold onto your hats because I've got another great activity for you:

Activity: *Three Questions – One Answer*

That's right, some more questions for you to answer. But these questions probe deeper than the previous ten, if only because they require a more lengthy answer. That's because all but one of the following questions will require more than mere "yes" or "no" answers, and each one is specifically designed to see where you are, right now, in relation to your breakthrough.

In this activity, you will be asking yourself three simple – but far from routine – questions:

- **Question # 1:** *In one word, right down how you feel about how you currently are?*
- **Question # 2:** *What Is the Biggest Problem I Want to Solve for Myself?*
- **Question # 3:** *What Does My Breakthrough Look Like?*

These questions pose bigger challenges than the first set, so take more time this time. Even when writing a one-word answer, think about it more than you might a typical "yes" or "no" response. Oftentimes we slip into automatic mode when taking these exercises; do your best to avoid that here.

This is a true "self-help" book in that you are the only one who can help yourself. I can guide you, inspire you, poke you and prod you but, ultimately, you are the one who is going to have to make the tough choices. I want this book to be an opportunity for you to learn something new about yourself, to get to know yourself better than ever before and to challenge yourself in bigger, bolder ways.

Fortunately, these questions will accomplish all that – and so much more:

Question # 1: *In one word, right down how you feel about how you currently are?*

Can you describe your current situation in one word? Can you look at your life and sum it up in a single emotion? It's important for you to try because this is part of the exercise. Sometimes the more words we use, the less they mean. When we are occasionally forced to strip away all our fancy words and use just a single one to describe a person, an emotion or a moment, we have to think carefully about which word we use – and why it describes it so perfectly.

And that's the point here; think hard about that one word. Mull it over, try it out, put it away and try something else then come back to it and compare/contrast until you've found just the right fit.

I feel your pain, because I know that this was a challenging question for me, personally, to answer. It still is. And if I was being completely honest with myself when I woke up at 4:30 that one fateful morning, the picture didn't look very pretty, or so I thought at the time. I like to say that you can lie to others, but you can't lie to yourself. No one is looking over my shoulder; no one is reading my journal. I can say what I want to say, right here and right now.

So the one word that describes where I was at the time is "STUCK". Not moving forward, not moving back, just… stuck. Stranded in neutral, grinding my gears, hustling, hustling, and never getting anywhere. Have you ever just felt stuck? Like you're not really getting anywhere, no matter how hard you spin your wheels? Like you're not getting anywhere you want to go? Not even close? Like you're just stuck in time, treading water, with no land in sight?

I heard a quote once that said, "If you're not growing, you're dying." That's what stuck feels like; dying a little bit every single day. After all the failures – or at least what I perceived to be failures in my mind – you get to a point that you become "gun shy" about moving forward.

Where you're not sure what to do anymore, not sure what people think of you, or even how you think about yourself. You're afraid to try anything new because everything you've tried so far has failed. At least, that's how it feels when you're stuck.

And if you stay stuck long enough, if you stay down long enough, eventually you start to lose confidence in yourself. You start becoming a follower instead of the leader that you have always been.

You don't just second guess the big decisions, you literally second guess everything: what to wear to a meeting, whether to go to the meeting, what you'll say when and if you do get there, and how many different ways you could screw it up! You become more cautious in making choices because you don't want to move in the wrong direction ever again, which of course keeps you from going in *any* direction.

That is how you end up stuck: too afraid to go back to where you've been, too afraid to risk going anywhere else for fear it will send you back farther down than you already are. Fear keeps you stuck; fear of the unknown, fear of failure, fear of… *fear*.

Sadly, fear starts when we're very, very young and, if we're not careful, we'll be its victims all our life. Our parents and teachers – who I'm sure only wanted the best for us – taught us from day one that failure is wrong and that only success matters. All we ever heard while growing up is how bad it is to fail. You always had to get good grades; you had to be at the top of the dean's list, the leader of the pack, the head of the class.

"Don't attempt something if you can't win at it!"

"If you can't stand the heat, stay out of the kitchen!"

"Go big or go home!"

No offense to any of my teachers growing up but, as a mature adult I now recognize that these statements are completely and utterly false. Failure doesn't always mean a step back. In some cases, it may even mean a step forward. That's right: you *can* fail your way to success, one screw-up, blunder or risk at a time. The only way that you become a failure in business – and in life – is by quitting; is by just plain giving up and no longer trying.

If you keep trying, there is at least a chance of success, no matter how slim. And the more you try, the greater the odds of success become. But if you quit, if you simply give up, there IS no chance of winning the game because you are simply no longer *in* the game.

Don't get me wrong: failure is never fun. It hurts to fail – it hurts a lot! And, like I said, it makes you gun shy about moving forward because, well, once bitten, twice shy and all that. No one likes to fail, but I have it on good authority – i.e., my own – that failure is not the end of the world. In fact, when viewed in the proper perspective – in terms of a potential Breakthrough – failure can be just the beginning.

I have had many failures in life, but I have also had a lot of success. In fact, objectively speaking, the successes far outweigh the failures. In fact, if I listed all my successes, it would sound a whole lot like bragging. And yet it's perfectly okay for me to go on and on about how I've failed.

Why is that? Why are we so preoccupied with the few times we've failed versus the many, many times we've succeeded? The problem with many of us – I would even go so far as to say most of us – is that we tend to focus on our failures, not our successes. And I think a lot of that "stinking thinking" about failure over success goes back to how we were raised, in that "if you're not the winner, you're a loser" mentality.

If you think about our lives, most of us are already a success story. Just putting a roof over our heads, paying the bills and putting groceries in the fridge each week, in this day and age, is a monumental task! To say nothing of whether or not you may have actually achieved any kind of academic, creative, professional, financial or leadership success.

But it's human nature, I believe, to want more, no matter how much we may have. Success can be addictive. It's a great feeling to succeed, and it's okay to want more; to be an overachiever to the point where we want to be the boss, and not just the employee; own the company, own two companies, and own stock in several more.

We want to set goals for ourselves and reach them, but we often beat ourselves to a pulp if we fail along the way, even just a little. That's what I caution against – not failure itself, but failing in the attempt at greatness. And what is greatness? What is failure? What is success? I believe it's all relative, that your thoughts determine your actions and your actions determine your results and, as we'll learn later in this book, that your mindset ties all of this together to create a purposeful, powerful Breakthrough.

That is, if you'll let it.

If we would simply look at our lives in perspective, objectively, we will often find that we are more successful than we believe ourselves to be. What is it about human nature that we dwell on our flaws and failures – we're ten pounds overweight, not six feet tall, not rich enough, thin enough, handsome enough, etc. – instead of all the wonderful, awesome, great and positive qualities that we do have?

Think about how much happier, healthier and successful we might be if we simply closed our eyes, counted to ten and saw our lives from a new perspective? If we filtered out the failures and focused on the successes? If we ignored those ten or twenty extra pounds and focused on how fashionable, friendly and talented we are? I believe if we could do so, so much of what we accomplish in life would fall into the "success" category versus the "failure" column.

The thing about failure and success is that they are often two sides of the same coin. In fact, some successes are a direct result of our past failure(s). Take this book, for example. I have been trying to write this book for over four years and now, because I didn't quit, here we are!

I stopped, I started, I wrote a little, I waited a lot, I inched forward and crept back and finally prevailed. But every time I started, stopped and gave up… it felt like a failure. I would beat myself up and walk away and figure I'd never pick it up again because, well, if I couldn't get it right the first time, if I couldn't hit a home run out of the park the first time up at bat, why bother? At one point I thought I'd never finish this book, and yet something kept bringing me back around to it for one more try.

I have literally started this book at least a dozen times and the title has changed at least *eight* times. It's been called "A Sum of All Parts," "Become a Better U" and even "Become a Richer U," to name just a few. So had I stopped writing this completely then, yes, I would have failed, but because I decided that it was time to finish I had a Breakthrough, and so will you.

You just have to keep failing forward!

Question # 2: *What Is the Biggest Problem I Want to Solve for Myself?*

This second question caused me to think a whole lot because my mom always said, "Be careful what you ask for, words have power and you just might get it!" That being said, my first thought about how I might solve my "biggest problem" would be more money!

I mean, what *wouldn't* one or five or even *ten* million dollars solve, right? No more money worries, never hustling to pay the rent or the mortgage, cars paid off, kids can go to any college they want or, if not, never work again. But being a bit more realistic, is money the *only* thing that can make me happy? Is it the answer to all my problems? Will it solve everything, just like that, in the blink of an eye?

The answer to that is "No!"

One of my favorite authors, Jim Rohn, once said something that has always stuck with me: "Don't wish the problem would be smaller, ask for more skills to solve your problems." So by that logic, if someone was to just "give" me money and it eventually ran out, I would have no idea on earth how to replenish it again.

Since I had no part in earning it – used no skills, talents, smarts or know-how to get it – how could I ever hope to repeat it? I think that's what happens to a lot of those lottery winners who seem to always wind up broke after running through millions and millions of dollars in just a matter of years.

They think money is everlasting and, when they find out that it really isn't, how do they make more? After all, the only skill they used to earn it in the first place was picking a few random numbers out of a hat. How do you repeat that in one lifetime?

Unfortunately, I'm not alone because I've found that most people tend to answer "money" to this question. (In fact, ask most people any question and they'll answer, "More money!") And why not? After all, that's the fastest, most immediate, most instant solution to their problems – to any of their problems.

We all want a quick fix; the sooner, the better. That's because we live in a society of instant:

- We have a microwave oven because we want that food **instantly**;

- We have "fast acting" remedies because we can't wait for that headache, sinus congestion, indigestion or aches or pains to go away naturally and want relief **instantly**;
- We have cell phones because we want to connect **instantly**;
- We have computers to get information **instantly**;
- We want to shop online because we want that shopper's high **instantly**;
- We want to buy a song, download and listen to it **instantly**;
- Forget the library or bookstore, let me download that bestseller and read it on my iPad, tablet, Nook or Kindle **instantly**;
- We watch on-demand movies because we want our entertainment **instantly**.

And that's all well and good. Later in this book you'll read about the power of speed, how faster is actually better and a lot of this "instant" technology can actually help us Breakthrough sooner rather than later. This is not a jab at speed, it is a comment on how faster isn't always better. How, in fact, sometimes waiting for something can actually teach us to appreciate that something more than if we simply got it at a fast-food drive thru and consumed it immediately.

But somewhere along the way we forgot the simple joys of waiting for a package to arrive, of roasting a chicken and savoring its fresh, home-cooked aromas and taste, the anticipation of waiting for the next Harry Potter book to arrive and standing in line with our friends to be one of the first ones to read it, of waiting until next week to see the cliffhanger ending of last week's TV show or even taking a nice, long walk to get rid of our headache the natural way.

Instant may be convenient, but as a country – as a planet – we're getting to the point where we can't wait for a 30-minute pizza delivery anymore, let alone the kind of ultimate, outlier, Breakthrough success this book promotes.

We also forgot about bigger issues, like paying our dues, earning respect, learning the ropes and working hard to achieve something. That feeling of pride we felt when after all that hard work, blood, sweat and tears we actually accomplished something that no one could take from us.

Never underestimate the power, satisfaction and sense of pride of earning your keep, the joy of a job well done or the simple satisfaction of looking back at something worthwhile that you've accomplished and thinking, "I did that. That was all me."

Case in point: when I got my first black belt in Taekwondo, it was a feeling like no other I have ever experienced since. The amount of hours that went into reaching that goal, the training involved, the discipline I had to summon, the pain I endured, the sheer willingness needed to finish, made this task that much sweeter once I finally achieved it. It's something no one can ever take away from me, and a lesson in perseverance that I'm glad I finally earned.

There is no monetary value to a black belt, but there are no amount of words to describe the strength, fortitude and resilience it gave me by merely sticking it out when many, many times I wanted to throw in the towel and give up on my goal. These kinds of invisible yardsticks are how we measure our own success. Not in dollars and cents, but in satisfaction, pride and contentment.

What if that's missing from a life? What if there is never an instance of sticking something out, hustling till it hurts, showing up early, staying late and generally going above and beyond the job description to reach a goal that is extremely significant, if only to yourself.

I'm no politician, professor or psychiatrist, but I look at the world today and I see children growing up with instant gratification in every single moment of their life:

- They have video screens in the back of the front seats so they don't even have to wait to get home to watch TV;
- They have a cell phone from the minute they learn to talk so they never have to be out of touch, calm, quiet or silent;
- They learn, from the earliest age, on computer screens that leap, jump, shout and play at the touch, swipe or tap of a finger;
- They have computers in class and can barely write cursive, let alone an entire book report, in longhand;
- At their part-time jobs their cash registers and phones calculate every figure for them;
- They are literally powerless without their smart phones, tablets, laptops, earphones and text messaging…

Why? Because it's all instant. Learning is instant. Knowledge is instant. School is instant. Money is instant. Checking is instant. Grading is instant. Music is instant. Books are instant. TV and movies are instant.

45

Now, I'm all for progress, technology and convenience, but what's going to happen to this generation of kids when they don't instantly, immediately and perfectly get the first job they go for? How is a lifetime of instant gratification preparing them for that first big disappointment in life, be it personal, professional, academic or, God forbid, financial?

Unfortunately, I don't think life *is* preparing this current generation for those kinds of challenges. I think our nation's children are in for a rude awakening when they begin the tough life lessons that so many of our generation – or at least *my* generation – take for granted.

I was reading a book about Millennials the other day and it was truly sobering to hear how an entire generation – raised on cell phones and Twitter and downloads and Netflix and smart phones and texting and Vines and Wi-Fi – simply can't abide "waiting" around to earn a promotion. It's bad enough taking an entry-level job, but if they don't achieve a leadership role in record time, say less than a year, they will simply move on and seek it at another company.

But what about ownership, pride of accomplishment, team work and brand loyalty? I fear for a generation that doesn't know the value of patience, and not as a virtue but as an actual learning tool that actively, directly and eventually leads to future success.

Absolutely if you're not being appreciated, or are genuinely undervalued in your present company, don't invite further abuse or waste more time by spending good effort after bad. But few of us can expect immediate gratification, in every role, at every company, every time!

Going back to our question, if I was to answer what the biggest problem I want to solve for myself is, then I would have to say it would be… to become better, to be able to stick with things longer, to have more wisdom to make better choices, to stop procrastinating, to decide what's important to me and go achieve it, to find patience to go through the journey instead of wanting it instantly.

Rather than money, I feel like these tools are going to prepare me for a stronger, smarter, more profitable life in the long run. What about you? What is the biggest problem you want to solve for yourself, and how will you go about doing just that?

Question # 3: *What Does My Breakthrough Look Like?*

Breakthroughs are like fingerprints; each one is identical to its owner. Your Breakthrough will not be my Breakthrough will not be your neighbor's Breakthrough or your spouse's Breakthrough or your child's. We own, possess and radiate a certain power and potential and that, as much as any other factor, will help determine how, when and even why we ultimately Breakthrough.

Likewise, everyone is reading this book for his or her own reasons. Maybe you're looking to have a better relationship with your spouse or child. Maybe you're looking for a new career. Maybe you're looking to switch college majors, get your MBA or your Ph.D. Maybe you're an inventor, entrepreneur or software designer and want to branch out on your own. Or maybe you're just stuck in neutral and don't know how to switch gears, or even which direction to go once you finally pop the clutch!

Whatever your reason for reading this book may be, your Breakthrough is personal to you, as it should be. There is no one size fits all Breakthrough you can simply buy off the rack, copy, paste or emulate. You have to do the work and be honest with yourself to determine what the life you always wanted for yourself looks like.

I believe that we all have three different versions of our lives – the past, the present and the future – and that you choose to live in whichever life you want, whether consciously or subconsciously, whether on purpose or by default. Let me explain: let's say that, in your past life, maybe there was some event, some defining moment, that you felt shaped you, made you who you are today.

Now, that past life could be great because you might not have all the problems you have now. You might have been the captain of the football team, or head cheerleader, maybe you were class president or simply experienced a period of a few months or a few years there where you had no job problems, no money problems and had no responsibility for anything whatsoever.

Whatever the situation, time period or reason, somehow – some way – you were made to feel safe and you have great memories of that one particular era. It could be high school, it could be college, it could be your first apartment, first job, first girlfriend, first car, whatever. The problem is, many of us get stuck in the past, always reliving the good old days while ignoring the present, let alone the future.

It's tempting, I know, to live in that safe, comfortable era where we felt cushioned, or complete or carefree, but as we will soon see there is danger in too much comfort, and life only really begins when you leave your comfort zone. And yet, this is where many people cling: to the comfortable, the safe, the carefree… the past.

We all know that one guy who starts every single conversation with, "I remember when I… so and so." Hey, you might even *be* that person… I'm just saying! But you can't move forward if you're always living in the past, talking about those "glory days" and cursing the life you lead in the present simply because it isn't the past – and forget about the future.

In my own case, I used to talk about how successful my investment firm was and how I used to take the whole staff on trips to Vegas, and how we were earning over $70,000 a month. I bragged about my overhead being over $30,000 a month in spending. It was like a badge of honor, tossing out those figures and wearing them on my chest like battle scars. Looking back on this, all I can think now is how stupid I was then!

Talk about living in the past! I wish I could go back in time and get my money back!!! I would do so many things differently if I could only go back then with what I know now and think, act and speak differently. Treat others differently, treat myself differently, put more emphasis on the right things instead of the big, bad, fast, fancy, flashy things.

But how much of life is like that? How many of us would do high school differently if only we knew how little being cool meant, and how important it was to just be ourselves, look around, take it easy and enjoy the experience as it happened?

Part of the reason many of us choose to live in the past is because we either didn't know how good we had it back then, or thought we had it good for all the wrong reasons. But by the time the past is in the past, we've already moved on and are stuck somewhere else hurrying through a present that will soon be the past as well.

If we treat every day as worthy of our attention and earnest application, then we won't need to live in the past because the present will be so exciting and full of Breakthroughs! But try telling me that back then!

But then one day I realized that, because I was always living in my past, not only could I not live in the present – let alone enjoy it – but I couldn't move forward into my future, either. What was next? I had no idea, because I was always looking in my rearview mirror at what I'd just left behind, not at the road ahead.

This brings me to my next life, which is the present life. Now, this could be good or bad for you, depending on your circumstances. This is the life as you see it now. Be honest with yourself and discuss what's good about now and what's bad about the life you're currently living.

Tell yourself all the things that are happening in your present life; the good, the great, the bad, the really bad, the ugly and the hideous. Is the reason you're preoccupied with the past because you can't stand the present you're actually living in? Is the reason you can't imagine a better future because you feel like you screwed up your past and your present so bad, there's simply no hope left for you?

For me, I am the most focused I have ever been living in the here and the now. My present is active, it's beneficial, it's clear, it's focused, it's here and it's now. I have a clear direction of what I want and how to achieve it, but with that being said, no matter how proud or excited I am about my present, I'm still not at the same financial or success status that I would like to be!

Then again, is anybody? Ever?

We always want more, don't we? Enough is never good enough, we want more, more, always more. More what, though? More everything! More time, more freedom, more money, more hours in the day, more savings in the bank, more daylight, more nightlife, more sleep, more energy, more prospects, more sales… just plain more. As satisfied as I am in the present, I am guilty of that right now. I feel that my drive and determination has finally met up with my focus. I had a Breakthrough and my present life is on its way to my future life, and that's where the fun really starts!

See, my future life is amazing. I love my past and my present, but my future life? This is the life I want and deserve. It's the life that I have been destined for. It's where all the struggles I've endured, all the hard work I've put in, all the hustle and swagger have finally paid off. In your future life, you know what to dream to make it exactly how you want it. Napoleon Hill said, "Whatever your mind can conceive and believe, the mind can achieve."

Do you believe that? I do. I've talked to many successful, amazing, thriving, creative, powerful, industrious and flourishing folks, and they almost all talk about the power of dreams. Not of the sleeping kind, but the kind that propel them to create a life where all the things they've ever imagined in their heads truly exist in the real world.

Dreams are not just for the rich and powerful, but the rich and powerful live their dream life because they dared to dream a better life. They believed in the power of dreams – in the power of their dreams – and created a future life out of sheer determination, hard work and many, many Breakthroughs. And you can, too!

So start dreaming! How will you ever know when you arrive at your future life, if you don't know what it looks like beforehand? Descriptive visualization is a powerful tool. Have you ever tried it? Have you ever tried picturing something so strongly, so purposefully, so vividly that you could actually close your eyes and describe it with the rest of your senses?

Be vivid and detailed in your descriptions. You should know exactly – down to the colors and the fabrics and the brand names and the consistency – what your future looks like. Be able to feel the leather of your executive desk chair, smell the "new car smell" of that BMW, touch that cold marble floor of your new office building, feel the plush carpet of your new home between your toes.

No detail is too small to be overlooked in your purposeful and powerful visualization of a bright future – the brightest future possible – for yourself. I had a colleague who used to visualize his future down to the letterhead on his stationary, down to the stock art on his business card, down to the music he'd play while customers were on hold at his 1-800 number – down to what his 1-800 number would actually be!

Those powerful, purposeful and vivid visualizations helped him start his own company and reach Breakthrough status in a very big way. It wasn't just picturing the stock art for his business card or urban contemporary jazz on his hold music, but those realistic, sensual and vivid details helped breathe life into his dreams as surely – as powerfully – as any of the other learning tools he applied to his own personal success story.

Your future is waiting for you to create it, but first you have to believe it, and often we need to see it before we'll believe it. So be specific in what you want. Know *exactly* what you want because you have already visualized it, very, very specifically, time and time again. Focus, look and see the life you want to lead and then take active steps to make that life happen.

I am no stranger to active visualization. In fact, it's one of my favorite past times. (More on this later!) For me, I know exactly what my future life looks like because I have literally pictured it hundreds and thousands of times: I'm speaking to 60,000 people who have paid to see me talk in a giant arena! I have been featured and interviewed by *Success* magazine for their cover story. I have a million dollars – liquid – in my personal checking account. I have the number 1 bestseller on the New York Times bestseller list and in all the top categories on Amazon.com.

I have a private helicopter that takes my family and me in and out of the city from our private, obscure home in Northern California. I'm able to send my wife on a shopping spree once a month in New York and Paris. I spend as much time with my kids as they want without me worrying about work. This is my future life, my Breakthrough life, the life I was destined to have.

The life I *will* have.

Notice how the details are powerful and specific. It's not just a few people in a hotel conference room, it's 60,000 people in a stadium. I can picture the stadium, hear the feedback on the microphone as I take to the stage, feel the roar of the crowd as I pace the stage in front of them.

It's not just any magazine, it's *Success* magazine. It's a full-on profile, just like I've read of other smart, fabulous, creative and successful people. It's the cover story, and I'll have it blown up and framed and hang it on my office wall.

It's not 100 million dollars in my checking account, or 10 million, it's one million. I know that doesn't sound like a lot, but I like to visualize the real, the powerful, the actual, things that could actually, truthfully, terrifically happen to me. There may be ten million in investments, even 100 million in real estate and property and stocks and options, but a million in the bank – liquid and ready at a moment's notice – that's more than enough for me!

Even the helicopter? That's not as much as you might think and, yes, I have priced it because I take my guided visualization very, very seriously. (And so should you!)

So, what does your Breakthrough life look like?

Wait, don't answer until you read the next chapter:

Action Steps for Chapter 2

Before you get started using the lessons I've shared in Chapter 2, ask yourself these simple questions:

Do you know where you are?

Are you in a good place to move forward?

If not, what can you do to get in a better place?

Do you understand your past, present and future life?

How do you feel about your past life?

What is good – or bad – about your present life?

Do you have a solid visualization in mind for your future life?

Chapter 3:
The Second Strategy – What's Holding You Back?!?

"You can conquer almost any fear if you will only make up your mind to do so. For remember, fear doesn't exist anywhere except in the mind."
- Dale Carnegie

So, we've determined where you are in your past, present or future life, even where you want to go when you decide to Breakthrough. Now we need to discover why you're not already there. In other words, what's holding you back from reaching your true, full potential? Why do you feel unhappy – or anxious or dissatisfied – about where you are? Why are you so uncertain about your future?

The fact is, most of us have big dreams, but experience slightly smaller – in some cases *much* smaller – realities. We know we're not quite where we want to be, and yet we're not quite sure how to get where we want to go – or even if we're up for the journey.

There are a variety of reasons for that, as we've been discovering throughout this book so far, but to begin this next chapter I'd like to introduce you to one of life's biggest intimidators: fear.

Fear, Failure and You: *A Love Story*

That's right, fear. Statistics show that good, old-fashioned fear is one of the main reasons why most people don't succeed in life. Fear of failure, fear of success, fear of financial difficulties, fear of change, fear of discomfort, fear of facing the new or going back to the old. You name it, fear can kill it. I've seen fear, firsthand, so I know just how powerful it can be.

Honestly, for such a small word, *fear* has got to be one of the strongest, most powerful, most intimidating words in the English dictionary. People will become absolutely incapacitated by the sheer thought of doing something that they are afraid of. I'm not even talking about clinical phobias (such as fear of spiders, fear of heights, fear of driving, etc.), which are real and debilitating fears that cause complete isolation and paralysis; I'm talking about our everyday fears of simply getting… unstuck.

Moving on with life can be the scariest thing in the world for some people, which is how fear keeps us isolated, insulated, stuck in the same place, sometimes for years – sometimes forever. We can act tough and try to be brave and talk a good game but, subconsciously – maybe even consciously – fear wins because we've given it so much power it is literally stronger than our desire for change.

I have witnessed friends, family members, colleagues and clients – all very smart, talented, creative, passionate, purposeful people – lose brilliant opportunities and loads of potential simply because they can't imagine the thought of going to that next level and doing that one thing that makes them shake in their boots:

- **Pitch an investor;**
- **Draw up a business plan;**
- **Go for an interview;**
- **Go back to college;**
- **Start their own company;**
- **Apply for a loan;**
- **Etc.**

As a result, most people will never achieve their goals in life because of these four little letters: FEAR! (And I don't believe it's a coincidence that "fear" is a four-letter word!!!)

All my life I have watched good people, smart people wanting and wishing for more, but it never seems to come. For whatever reason, you check in with them from time to time and those plans they told you about last time you spoke, that project or that degree or that raise or that promotion, well, would you believe it? It just fell through.

And when you push a little harder, ask another question or two, it turns out they didn't fill out the paperwork that was necessary to enroll, or they missed a certain deadline, or didn't show up for an interview, or in some way, form or fashion just... dropped the ball.

Why? Why do such smart people always seem to sabotage such great opportunities? Why are they always stuck in neutral, even though they know perfectly well how to drive? Well, I believe that most people are simply scared to push past what's holding them back and, as a result, they give up before they even get started.

They've grown comfortable and complacent in life and, even though they're vaguely dissatisfied, or even actively searching for something different because they know they should, they just can't untangle themselves from fear's mighty grip.

It happens to all of us, I believe, at some point or another. We know something is keeping us from the life we've always dreamed about, and what that "something" is, is simply too scary to contemplate – so we don't. We just stop pulling at that thread altogether. Instead we content ourselves with the knowledge that life is "good enough," never admitting that we yearn for something more.

Stuck in Neutral

I believe that most of us have been programmed to think a certain way, a vaguely anxious, uncertain and fearful way, and that this programming is very hard to undo. It's not like computer software we can dump, delete and then load on a new program and start fresh with a brand new operating system that is absolutely fearless. This programming is hardwired right to our personality, and it not only shapes who we are, but who we are destined to become.

This programming starts at a very early age, when we are first told that failure is a bad thing, and that no matter what, we always have to win at all costs. "You need to be the best," we are told, by our parents, our teachers, our coaches, our mentors and even our classmates, teammates and friends. (All, I believe, with the best of intentions.) "Strive for greatness and nothing else," they tell us. "Only your best will do, and only the best deserve to win."

With all of this pressure to become the best – and the harsh realities that come along with dominating a field, any field – we're doomed to fail. Even if we succeed 99 times and fail only once, we've still failed. That's what we've been taught, that's what we believe, and no one can sway us from the grim reality that we're a failure. Given that "do or die," "all or nothing" mentality, it's no wonder that most people quit trying after failing a time or two.

They are too fearful of not accomplishing their secret, hidden goal that they settle for not even trying to make it a reality. After all, if they go for it and fail (again), what will all those people think:

- *What will my friends say if I come back home after trying – and failing – to make it in the big city?*
- *They all knew I was up for that audition. If I come back home now, I'll be the laughing stock.*
- *I won't get that promotion, no way. And then I'll have to explain to my Dad why I'm such a loser.*
- *All those other candidates are way better than me. At least if I keep this job, I won't have egg on my face…*

And on and on it goes, a repeating loop, a vicious cycle, a whirl of negative self-talk that can't help but congratulate itself every time we given into that unspoken fear that drives our mindset and fuels our choices.

When faced with that almost blinding fear of failure, sometimes it can just seem a whole lot easier to put our head in the sand and settle for average. Blend into the mediocrity of society, get a good job, make a paycheck, pay the mortgage and call it a day. It's safe there, it's well within our comfort zones and we never have to worry about letting anyone down, or care what others think about us, because in our own little corner of the world, we know we can succeed.

We don't even have to worry about what we think of ourselves. Well, if that's okay for you, then this book is probably *not* for you. Why? Because this book is about you wanting and believing you deserve more. It's about learning the 7 Strategies to Help You Unlock Your Greatest Potential and then actually using them to, you know… Unlock Your Greatest Potential!

It's about you having your future life:

Looking Backward; Moving Forward: *Fulfilling Your Future Life*

After the last chapter you should have a better understanding of where you are in your past and even present life, and also what your "future life" looks like. Remember your future life? That was the one where you had a strong, clear and vivid picture of the life you want to lead. It's the life you can build for yourself, with no walls or horizons, no limits or guardrails, a completely blank canvas on which to paint your future life's greatest masterpiece.

However you picture it, whatever you imagine for yourself, use your future life like a lighthouse, shining forth in the darkness of your present life, guiding you where you want to be. You might not know the exact path forward but, if you keep a clear vision of your future life in front of you at all times, you can get there eventually. But ignoring your future life, or forgetting or neglecting it, leaves you in the dark with nothing to guide you.

Talk about being "stuck"!

But that's not you. I know because you're still here, reading these words, and that means you've taken my advice and already have a clear, decisive picture of your future life in your head. You know what it looks like, and now I'm going to help you get there.

So now that we know what your future life looks like, we need to find out how to break through the fear, the procrastination and the stories that we tell ourselves, which debilitate us from moving forward and achieving our goals.

One step toward your future life is to remember that success is a series of events, not one single occasion. Case in point: I heard somewhere that a baseball player swings and misses 7 out of 10 times at bat.

Imagine that!

In any other world, that failure to success ratio would be considered a huge failure. Imagine not closing 7 out of every 10 sales, or missing 7 out of every 10 deadlines at work. You'd have been fired a long, long time ago! But think about it: those three hits every ten times at bat still has that player hitting a 300 average, which makes him millions of dollars every year.

If you think long and hard about that statement for a moment, then you must also realize that you don't have to hit every time you're at bat to win, either – just a small percentage of the time. In fact, every time you succeed just a little, you chip away at the notion that one failure equals permanent failure. And if you actually open up and talk to people, like a mentor or your mastermind group (more on them later), you will learn that the most successful people you know have also failed more times than the average person.

Why? Because the more you try, the more you will fail. Talk about averages; that's basic math. The more you swing, the more you're likely to miss. The more you submit, the more you're likely to get rejected. But if you hit just three times out of every ten, if you just get one editor to like what you've submitted, you're still a success.

But we don't want to hear that. Like I said earlier, we've all been taught that you have to get a home run, grand slam, hit it out of the park every single time to bat or you are going to be considered the world's biggest loser. This statistic proves that that mindset simply isn't true, and I hope it's given you comfort that even millionaire athletes still get paid to fail.

It's actually part of their job description.

Telling Stories: *A Guide to Your Future Self*

Sometimes in life it's not about hitting a home run every time you step up to the plate, but simply getting up to bat in the first place. That way, hit or miss, walk or foul out, at least you tried.

And yet, time after time, we tell ourselves the wrong story about winning and losing, about success and failure, and in particular about our own self-worth. By the wrong "story," I mean that negative self-talk that drags us down instead of builds us up.

And it is very much a story, and we're writing it, speaking it and telling it all day long, every single day. From the minute we get up in the morning until the moment we fall asleep at night, our internal dialogue is spinning a tale that has been woven together from the tiny bits of our conscious and subconscious self-talk.

Once upon a time I thought my mind was my friend, but after paying closer attention to the story I was telling myself every day, I realized that, in fact, my mind – my very own mind – was my own worst enemy.

It told me the most horrible things about myself, from morning to night, so that if I didn't want to believe it, I had to actively fight what my brain was telling me:

- *"You can't write a book; you're a bad speller."*
- *"They won't hire you, you never finished college."*
- *"They won't invest with me; I'm not the right color or age."*
- *"You can't do that; it's never been done."*
- *"They will never listen to me, I'm nobody."*
- *"They will never follow me, I haven't hit it big."*

And on and it went, until I decided to put a stop to it and start telling myself a different "story". But it wasn't easy, because like I said, we've been telling ourselves the same bad story for as long as we can remember. This negative storytelling does us no favors when we say things to ourselves like, "There's no way you'll get that job/promotion/loan/degree/<u>fill in the blank</u>, so why even bother?"

Why does this happen? In a word, fear. Our brain's natural instinct is to keep us safe, always, so it keeps us in line by keeping us comfortable, home and safe.

How does this help? It doesn't. We can't Breakthrough if we don't even believe we're worth it!

Who does this help? No one. Not a single person, and that's what's so harmful about it.

And yet, time after time, we as reasonable, smart, intelligent adults listen to this "bad" storytelling instead of our instinct, which of course says, "Go for it! Who are you kidding? You're great for that job/promotion/loan/degree/<u>fill in the blank</u>, so what are you waiting for?"

Think of how great life could be, of how we could reach our unlimited potential, if only we could rewrite our internal self-talk and tell ourselves a brand new story, one where we're finally the hero, and not the same crummy bad guy, over and over and over again.

Wouldn't that be nice?

So why is it that we listen to the stories that do us no good over those that might help inform, inspire and support our future lives? Why do we feed the negative self talk and starve the positive reinforcement? I believe that we listen to the stories that feed our fear. Remember, fear is the greatest challenge to our hopes, our dreams and our future lives imaginable.

And yet fear keeps us comfortable, safe from trying, and so we subconsciously reward it by listening to what it says to us. When it tells us "no," we listen. When it tells us we "can't," we agree. We may not want to, we may even fight it and struggle for awhile but, in the end, we find that giving in is simply the path of least resistance. It's easier to give into fear and stay safe and comfortable because to fight our fear means discomfort, anxiety and something else: potential.

That's why we need to take the pen, the typewriter and the computer keyboard back from fear and begin writing our own stories again. We must first acknowledge our fears – whatever they may be – and then face them so that we know who we're talking to when we say good things about ourselves.

So, what stories do YOU tell yourself when it comes to your future life? When I was trying to think about what's been holding me back all these years, I started by asking myself a few questions over and over again:

- **What are the stories you are telling yourself?**
- **What is the one thing you are most fearful of?**
- **What did you experience that brings on this fear?**
- **How does this one fear debilitate you from moving forward?**
- **What's holding you back from your big Breakthrough?**
- **What the worst thing that can happen?**

Dr. Shad Helmstetter wrote a great book called *What to Say When You talk to Your Self* (Park Avenue Press, 2011).What I love about this book is it makes you consciously stop and think of the constant programming many of us have gone through all of our lives in order to understand that it's not our fault we think this way. We have literally been programmed to fail.

I believe on some subconscious level we all know that we've been conditioned to want the best, but fear the rest. What this book and so many others do is make us stop and actively think about why we think, reason and fear the way we do.

This programming begins early on. Think back on your childhood and you are likely to recall dozens of times when your mind was conditioned – or programmed – to think a certain way. From how we put on our shoes in the morning – both socks first, then shoes, then tie shoes or one sock first, then one shoe, tie that first then on to the next sock, the next shoe and tie that – stay with us pretty much forever.

If you don't believe me, try putting your socks and shoes on differently tomorrow and tell me how easy that is! But the psyche – and the programming – goes much deeper than mere shoe tying, bike riding or learning cursive or long division.

Particularly the negative things we experience as children – the name calling, the embarrassment, the shame, the humiliation, the bullying, the angry coaches or petty teachers – these things seem to last well into our adulthood. In fact, many of us never forget them.

Think back to your own childhood. Wasn't there someone who hurt you as a kid and you still remember it today as an adult? Vividly? Wasn't there a person that said something to you that hurt you when you were younger, and now you're destined to relive that moment over and over again as an adult?

Maybe a classmate that teased you, a kid who bullied you on the playground, a teacher who scolded you for not having the right answer, a parent that said you weren't good enough, or a spouse that took your strength away by being verbally abusive over the years. Any one of these instances are enough to scar us for life and, in the process, permanently alter and warp the stories we tell ourselves – *if* we're not careful.

Fate and Our Future Selves

Now step back and look at your past life differently. Imagine what life could be like if that painful event had never happened to you. Imagine how confident you might be today if you never had that ugly encounter from your childhood, youth, young adulthood or even recent past. Wipe the slate clean, even if it's only in your imagination, and imagine a life where that thing – that painful, ugly thing – never really happened.

Let's say that as a child, you had a teacher that made you give oral reports in class every Friday. Book reports, social studies reports, history reports, didn't matter, every Friday everyone in the class had to stand up and give a report. For some reason, or so it seemed, yours were never quite good enough.

It seemed no matter how hard you tried, you just never got it right. If you gave a book report, your teacher scolded you for saying the author's last name wrong. If you gave a history report, your teacher scolded you for leaving out an important date. And on and on. It got so bad that you started to dread Fridays and, because you dreaded them so much, subconsciously you became certain that you would always screw something up.

So, naturally, you did. How could you not? You were so focused on failure you couldn't allow yourself to succeed. You were so preoccupied with how you pronounced this name or that, or that you'd crammed in all the dates, that your voice choked or you broke out in flop sweat or you didn't sleep the entire night before and recited the report like one of the living dead. And, without fail, your teacher hammered you for it, right there in front of the class, every single Friday.

The experience left you so shaken that even years after you no longer had that teacher, every time you had to get up in front of a group of people, you froze, blanked, sputtered and choked. This single memory – this "story" that teacher told you, the one that said that you weren't good enough, smart enough, prepared enough, etc. – set you on a collision course with failure.

But it doesn't have to be that way. You're not in that class anymore. You're not in junior high or high school. You know how to speak to people, make eye contact, do your homework, get your facts straight and yet still you tell yourself the same story because it has been programmed into your brain a certain, specific and memorable way. You hear "speak in front of a group" and you freeze, already choking at the memory of that long distant class and the way that teacher made you feel.

I mentioned earlier that we are the sum of all of our parts, not just the good, not just the bad. Every piece of information we receive about ourselves – good, bad or indifferent, ugly or pretty, compliment or cut down – becomes a part of our subconscious DNA. So every time someone says something to you, whether good or bad, it gets locked away in our subconscious mind and when something comes up that "triggers" it, we recall an emotion that was attached to that certain memory.

If someone called us "fat" when we were reaching for a donut one time (and it only takes one time) and it made us feel really bad and self-conscious about ourselves, now every time we see a donut, pastry, baked good, etc., we will recall that unpleasant memory.

On the flip side, if someone called us "fit" after we just exercised, we will likely replay that pleasant memory every time we go to the gym or workout and that becomes the story we tell ourselves. Again, good or bad, the subconscious mind is so strong that it affects the story we tell forever, based on millions of internal and external clues that we input all through our lives.

Again, depending on whether the memory was good or bad, it will affect how we approach certain situations. How does the story affect, say, asking for a promotion at work or dining out with a client? Every memory feeds the stories we tell ourselves, often for the worst.

Change Your Mindset Change Your Story

I believe the stories we tell ourselves can be extremely debilitating, almost crippling, if we don't learn how to change our mindset, change our thinking and literally rewrite the way we talk to ourselves.

To realize the future self we have in mind for ourselves, we need to lose the negative stories and start telling ourselves positive ones. We can rewrite history, but it takes effort – constant and conscious effort.

No, you may never be able to "un-hear" what that teacher said about your oral reports, or that bully said about your physique, or that girl said about your breath, but you can undo the damage it's been wreaking on your life ever since. We like to think that our past determines our future, that our fates are sealed, that we were born a certain type of person and that to rock the boat and try to rewrite our carefully scripted roles can only lead to failure. That is patently, unbelievably and almost cruelly false. Don't be a slave to the past, just because it's comfortable, calming and your own; look to the future and begin undoing the damage of the past one day, one word, at a time.

Start by talking positively to yourself. You can do it! You really can! Forget the past for a moment; you can't do anything about it anyway. Instead, live in the present tense. See how it feels. I can tell you, it feels great.

Letting go of the past isn't easy, and like our shadows we're never fully rid of our own personal history. But when we disengage from that negative storytelling and begin to see today as a blank page upon which we can literally write anything, it opens up a whole new world of possibilities. And trust me, you are dwelling on something that means far more to you than it ever did to the person who harmed you.

In fact, that person may not even remember what happened that day they hurt you so badly. They may not even have meant to hurt you, and would in all likelihood feel horrible to think that they affected the rest of your life so adversely. Oftentimes the pain we feel for years, decades even, because of a sharp word, jab or cut down meant absolutely nothing to the person who hurt us in the first place.

I remember a friend telling me how this girl back in school once said, "Hurry up, Fatty!" in line behind her in the cafeteria. From that day forward, my friend brought her lunch to school and never bought food in the cafeteria line again. Ever. She lurked in the corners after that, eating alone, worried that this person would see her and start calling out names again.

She suffered for years and years until finally, at her 20-year high school reunion, she saw the girl – now a grown woman, they both were at this point – and somehow found the courage to explain how much that moment had hurt her back then. How it still hurt to this day. The woman looked back, stunned, and said, "I don't even remember saying that. And I certainly didn't mean it if I did. You were far from fat in high school, and you look great now!"

All those years of hurt, pain, heartache, shame and negative self-talk were the result of a throwaway comment the person never even remembered saying! It was as if the moment had never happened, but of course it happened for my friend and colleague in a very real and harmful way. Unfortunately, she let it happen over and over and over again.

You don't have to. Tell yourself another story; a positive one this time.

Instead of focusing on the negative all the time, try focusing on the positive. I know it's challenging to change our thinking, but it's possible. In fact, people do it all the time. One of my favorite mentors, Les Brown, says that if you have a problem that can be solved by man, then you simply **don't have a problem**.

I think of that statement a lot because, when you really stop to think about it, there are so many people in this world who are in worse positions in life then you will ever be. Think about how big this world is, how vast and diverse it is, how there are people in countries far, far from ours who will never experience the creature comforts we take for granted every single day. Think how hard some people work just to scrape by, and how thankless and unrewarding their jobs are, year in, year out.

Every time you get frustrated because you're not a CEO yet, think about how many people don't even have a job. Every time you get frustrated by your apartment, suburban house or townhome, think about folks who have no home, or indoor plumbing, or running water, or refrigeration or healthcare.

I could go on and, in fact, in the earlier chapter I did talk at length about the life I led, and lost, and all that I suffered as a result of external factors over which I had no control. Maybe, for you, that "story" can help in putting your own life into perspective.

The Law of Attraction and the Power of Storytelling

I had always heard about the Law of Attraction, or LOA. At first I didn't believe in that mumbo jumbo, even though it's been around me all my life. It wasn't until I started working on myself, and started working on becoming a better me, that I discovered the power of LOA.

I started reading all of these books and stories of successful people and the one thing they had in common was what they thought about and how their day to day actions were detected by their thoughts. After awhile I knew what I was doing wasn't working so I said, "Let's give it a try."

At first it was hard changing old habits. I would make statements like, "It's just my luck," or "It always happens to me" or "It can't get any worse." Wow, talk about needing to rewrite your story! Just writing these statements now – knowing what I know about LOA – literally makes me feel fearful of putting these thoughts out into the world and how they might come back to haunt me.

But when I did change my habits and started saying positive things like "I am attracting the right successful individuals in my life" or "I am financially free" or "I am a bestselling author on the New York Times list," I started to believe the things that I wanted and it shifted my thought process to taking the action needed to go into that direction. That, I believe, is the real power of trying something new and learning that it can improve your life: taking action toward the right direction. Don't be afraid to try something new, simply because, well… it's something new! I believe where there is smoke there is fire, and LOA has worked for so many people, I just had to give it a try.

And I'm so glad I did!

I believe there are basic misconceptions about the Law of Attraction based on the belief that merely "thinking it will make it so." But thinking without action is merely dreaming, and we all know that to make our dreams a reality we must apply a little – and sometimes a lot of – elbow grease.

I'm not saying thoughts alone will make it so, but what I am saying – from my own personal experience – is that those thoughts help you start to take action in the right direction. How can that be bad? How can anything that makes you act on your dreams, that pits the positive against the negative, be bad?

It's all about storytelling. Tell the right story, and you'll take the right actions. Take the right actions and you will move closer and closer to your Breakthrough life, one step at a time. It's not necessarily easy, but it's not rocket science, either. A dream plus action plus commitment plus perseverance eventually becomes a reality.

That is a proven formula that has been working for successful people from the end of time, and it all starts with words. Why? Because words are the fuel for our mindset and, as we'll learn later in this book, the right mindset is absolutely vital to creating your ultimate Breakthrough.

Never, ever, *ever* underestimate the power of words or, subconsciously, the power of thoughts (which are translated as words). I believe that everything we do is fueled by our thoughts, and that they consciously – or subconsciously – force us to act in certain ways. Think negatively – "They'll never hire me," "I'll never get into Harvard," "She'll never go out with me," "They'll never give me that loan" – and I can almost guarantee you with absolute certainty that your thoughts will drive negative actions. I said it: actions. Because of the way you think, you will act differently.

Case in point: picture two people going into a job interview. One consciously tells themselves a positive, future story about getting the job while the other is convinced – absolutely and positively – that they won't get the job. Ever, no way, no matter what they do. The first applicant has a positive attitude and acts positively, hopefully, appropriately, for someone who is going to get that job. It doesn't mean they will, automatically, secure the position; only that they act like they will (act as if).

He comes in hopeful, eager to please, confident in his abilities, on equal footing with the interview panel and eager to answer their questions to the best of his ability. He makes eye contact, because he's eager to follow along and knows that body language is a great asset during an interview. His body language is relaxed, he exudes confidence and can't help but make a positive, lasting impression when it comes time to make that hiring decision.

The negative person acts negatively, already accepting defeat before the decision is handed down. "Why am I even here?" he asks himself. "This is so pointless." He may be qualified, he may even be overqualified, but he acts unqualified and, nine times out of ten, that negative story will tell itself to anyone interviewing him that day.

It might show up in how he presents himself, reserved, quiet, anxious, distracted. It could translate into his verbal rhythms. Everyone else in the room might be upbeat but he's down, solemn, registering far below the normal vocal rhythm in the room.

Maybe he avoids eye contact because he knows the interview panel will only be able to read his negative, uncertain mind. Taken together, all of these negative actions – as a direct result of negative thoughts – present a picture that is very hard to take positively.

Would you want to hire that person, as described?

Just writing about him, I want to fire him already!

Many of us don't take action because something… unknown… is holding us back. We may not even know it's our negative energy, negative thoughts and negative storytelling unless we actively begin to examine why we're not moving in the right direction and start asking ourselves some very pertinent, very "why" questions:

- *__Why__ am I so afraid to try something new?*
- *__Why__ am I anxious all the time?*
- *__Why__ am I so angry?*
- *__Why__ am I not farther along than I am at the moment?*
- *__Why__ haven't I tried harder to reach my goals?*
- *__Why__ do I always sabotage myself?*
- *__Why__ can't I picture anything good ever happening to me again?*

Once you start asking yourself the right questions, then you can start talking to yourself in a positive manner to become your own cheerleader for a change. Imagine that: cheering yourself on rather than talking yourself down!

I can't begin to tell you the power of positive storytelling, how it's worked for me over the years and literally turned my life around. I could never have written this book if I didn't absolutely, positively, 100% rewrite my own negative self-talk about writing a book and begin speaking positively about the process, the words, the ideas, and the outline. You are reading these words right now because I chose to rewrite my own self-talk and finally began urging myself forward, instead of backward.

But it all starts with the conversations you have with yourself. You have to speak success into existence. This is, by far, the most important thing you have to learn if you want your Breakthrough. You simply cannot break through – not completely, not successfully – if your negative self-talk is holding you back. Inevitably, invariably, you will start to sabotage yourself until you go right back to that "stinking thinking" that made you so fearful, anxious and doubtful in the first place. That's because the power of words is so intense that the things we tell ourselves will physically either stop us in our tracks or push us forward to success.

See how it all starts with us? That teacher, bully, girlfriend, coach or parent might have scarred you for life with those negative comments, but we are the one still having the conversation to this day.

We are the ones choosing to take it out, dust it off and drag it back up every single morning, noon and night.

And that has to stop if we are ever to move forward and meet our future self.

The choice is ours; it always was. If we have the power to choose to dredge up the past, then we have the same power to ignore it and focus on the present instead. Believe that. Believe that you have the power and act "as if" until you actually feel the power and start to see it positively manifest itself in reality. Proof is powerful and the first time you turn your thinking around, it can show you it's possible – and then you're off and running.

Start facing your fears and becoming more positive by asking yourself, "What is the one thing I am most fearful of? What is that thing that stops me from moving forward, every time?"

When you go to answer these questions, what's the first thing that comes to your mind? That is usually the thing you are struggling with the most. It could be money, a relationship, your career, your confidence, your skills or even fear itself. It could be your health, your finances, your housing situation or a dozen more things, but identifying it truthfully and honestly – remember, no one is reading your journal over your shoulder – is the first step to writing that fear out of your new self speaking story.

Realizing that one fearful thing and getting past it so you can move forward is what's going to help you start down the road to taking action. When I first thought of this question, I'll admit it brought tears to my eyes. Remember how I said earlier that there are times in your past that have direct links to present emotions? Well, for me, it was being at one of the lowest points in my life.

We had just lost everything for a second time around, and my depression was so bad that I couldn't get out of bed. I could barely function at life, let alone try to earn a living. I saw my wife – the woman that I had promised to take care of when we married – sitting on the floor wrapping pennies to buy groceries. I remembered my seven-year-old son, Chance, breaking his piggy bank open to give us all his money to help pay bills.

Yes we got over that, as a family, but returning to that dark, depressing place was the fear that kept me from moving forward. I just couldn't risk putting my family through that again. I was so fearful of losing that I couldn't even try to win, and the story I told myself – of counting pennies and breaking piggy banks and going bankrupt – literally paralyzed me.

With much work, training, thought and power I have learned to turn that fear into my "Why," that positive thought and story that moves me to action every day. That something is stronger than my fear of not succeeding.

That's my story.

What's yours?

Action Steps for Chapter 3

Before you get started using the lessons I've shared in Chapter 3, ask yourself these simple questions:

What is the story you tell yourself?

Is it positive? Or negative?

What can you do, right now, today, to change that story so that it's a positive one?

Do you believe in the power of words?

Are you ready to start using words to improve your life today?

Chapter 4:
The Third Strategy – Dream Big

"Shoot for the moon and if you miss you will still be among the stars."
- Les Brown

I once read a quote that asked, "What would you attempt if you knew you could not fail?" What a powerful question, and one we don't quite ask ourselves enough. Imagine a "free pass" button that would allow you to hit every time you were at bat, write a bestseller every time you sat down at the computer, make a blockbuster movie or simply run a 4-minute mile!

The fact is, some people act like this - Every. Single. Day. They approach the world from a "win/win" perspective. Every deal, every client, every sale, every transaction, every promotion, every gig… they act "as if" they can't fail. That they will win, every time at bat.

Believe it or not, there was a time when you acted like this, too; it was called childhood. Do you remember when you were a kid? How big you used to dream? How anything – anything at all – was possible?

Daydream Believer

Growing up, we all wanted to be a superhero, princess, doctor, fireman and a spy – all at the same time. We would live at the Hall of Justice on top of mount Olympus and the only way we could get there was by riding our winged horse Pegasus or flying there in Wonder

Woman's invisible jet, whichever was fastest! At least this is what I dreamed about. And, oh yeah, let's not forget I wanted a flying car just like the Jetsons had, too.

What did you want when you were a kid? A pet tiger? A mountain made of chocolate? To score the winning run in the World Series? Your very own castle? Childhood is a time filled with dreams, with wonder, with innocence and, above all... with possibility.

We are taught that every child can become president, play for the NFL or NBA, own their own business or become a millionaire. Our parents and teachers and sponsors and mentors and coaches encourage us to no end. We take their words as gospel and act "as if" we can conquer the world.

Somewhere along the line, however, we grow up and we stop dreaming. More and more often, the rallying cry of "You can do anything you want" is replaced by more negative comments. Comments like:

- *"Get your head out of the clouds."*
- *"You're too much of a dreamer; you need to think about reality."*
- *"That's just a pipe dream, it will never really happen."*
- *"Are you for real? That could never happen to someone like you!"*
- *"In your dreams!"*
- *"That's just a dream; it will never come true."*
- *"When are you going to stop dreaming and get a real job?!?"*

What happens when we hear something enough, from enough people? Well, eventually, we start to believe it. If enough people say it, we figure, it must be true, right?

And over time we start buying into those kinds of statements, and stop dreaming, little by little. We still act "as if," just… not quite as often. Now whenever we go to apply for a job, or a college, a little voice inside our head repeats those dream killing lies:

- *"Get your head out of the clouds."*
- *"You're too much of a dreamer; you need to think about reality."*
- *"That's just a pipe dream, it will never really happen."*
- *"Are you for real? That could never happen to someone like you!"*
- *"In your dreams!"*
- *"That's just a dream; it will never come true."*
- *"When are you going to stop dreaming and get a real job?!?"*

And they start to come true! Suddenly, or perhaps we just never noticed before, we *don't* actually get every job we apply for! We *don't* get every promotion we ask for! We *don't* achieve every goal, climb every mountain or win every time we're at bat!

So there must be some truth to all that mess, right?

Ultimately, inevitably, we start to become what the world calls a "responsible" adult. We settle down, and settle in. We start doing what is asked of us, without "asking" why. We start to conform to society and the rules they tell us are socially correct.

And with each passing day, a dream or two of ours dies. The more society tells us to "grow up" or "settle down," we stop following our true passions, or believing in our inherent talents.

Maybe we quit going out on auditions, sending in manuscripts, going to photography classes or going for our MBA. Maybe we put our plans to move out to Hollywood or New York or Chicago or Atlanta on hold, and stick around our hometown just a little while longer.

With each added responsibility, our belief in ourselves – and our dreams – dies off. When we strive so hard to be "normal," to "fit in" and settle down, we lose a bit of what makes us unique – as individuals, as dreamers, as doers, as talents.

But conformity comes at a cost:

The Cost of Conformity: *A Life Less Different*

Here's what I know about growing up: throughout the years, with all of the millionaires and even billionaires I have met, I have noticed that each and every one of them has something a little "off" about them. By that I mean, they are not what you would consider the "norm".

They tend to be social misfits, eccentrics and nonconformists. They don't think like 99% of the population, and that's what makes them so special. Their minds are active, they have vivid imaginations, are extremely creative and value the power of visualization. Where you and I might see a vacant lot, they see a storefront, an ice cream parlor or their next corporate franchise.

Somehow, some way, they have retained that "inner child" who still believes the quote I started this chapter with: "What would you attempt if you knew you could not fail?"

They understand failure, have even tasted the sting of defeat, but somehow they manage to retain a positive attitude and an air of hopefulness about them. Above all, they believe in their dreams, regardless of what anyone may have told them.

They ignore the doom and gloomers who tell them what can't be done. Instead they see the possibility in what *can* be done. Dreams are a part of their daily lives because, in fact, their dreams are what got them to their success in the first place.

I'm not saying that we shouldn't be responsible adults, that we shouldn't grow up and even settle down, but don't do so just because others tell you that you should, and never do so if it costs you your dreams. You can still pay your bills, love your spouse, raise your children and not sacrifice what makes your heart beat a little bit faster every time you think about it. Do what your heart says you should do, regardless of the facts, logic or reasoning behind it. Handle your business, but always be in the business of reaching your bigger, dream-focused, future life goals.

Let yourself off the hook. Life doesn't have to be so serious, so often. Yes, there are challenges, obstacles and responsibilities in life, but being a grown up doesn't mean giving up. It's okay to be a little quirky, a little eccentric, and follow your passions. In fact, now more than ever, in a world full of cookie cutter, follow the leader success stories, the most passionate, the most electric, the most exciting and the most successful are those who stand out of the crowd and live life to the beat of their own drummer.

You need look no further than musicians Jay-Z and Dr. Dre, who have used their creative mojo and passion for innovation to create million dollar and, in the case of Dr. Dre with his recent sale of "Beats" to Apple, billion dollar entrepreneurial empires based on everything from apparel to restaurants to real estate to technology. Try achieving that level of groundbreaking success by conforming, growing up or giving up on your dreams. Try being that successful without being a little bit offbeat, off center and off the map.

If that's what it takes to be successful, sign me up. The best thing I have ever been taught by one of my mentors is to find someone that has what you want, does what you want to do or has succeeded in a field you're passionate about and study them. Do what they do, say what they say, act like they act. Successful people leave clues as to how they've succeeded, but not in neon; it's up to us to find them.

Studying Success

How? How can we discover the secrets of millionaire and billionaire success stories? The fact is, anything you ever wanted to learn about success is out there, just waiting to be discovered.

Did you know you can study success, leadership, goal setting, and positive thinking? You can Google any or all of these topics and you will find some article or book to read, lecture to listen to, audio or podcast to discover, video to watch or seminar workshop that you can attend.

Every day in this country there are consultants, coaches, mentors, thought leaders and experts who are willing, eager and able to share their expertise with you. These are passionate and purposeful people who have achieved a certain level of success and feel compelled to share how they did so with others.

They show you how you don't have to reinvent the wheel but, in fact, can fast forward through a lot of mistakes – and make some very wise choices – by avoiding what they did wrong and focusing on what they did right. All this while personalizing their experience to translate into your own successful life.

While podcasts, videos and even seminars tend to play to larger crowds, you can also find a more intimate, one-on-one experience if you look closely enough. That's because there are several people out there that are approachable and are willing to sit down and let you pick their brain for questions and answers and more.

They will let you interview them, which may seem outlandish when you consider what they've achieved in life, but think of it this way: most people will see it as a form of flattery, so why wouldn't they? Mentors are a great way to receive guidance and wisdom from those who share your same passions, but have perhaps traveled a little further down their road to success than you have.

The one piece of advice I would give about entering into a mentor relationship – and something that was not taught to me but that I eventually learned on my own – was to never come empty handed. What I mean by that is that successful people often shy away from mentoring others because it is so often a one-sided relationship, with the mentor doing all the giving.

To facilitate a more beneficial mentor-mentee relationship, always figure out how you can bring value to the table. Many successful people have individuals in their lives that will constantly want something from them – take, take, take. You will separate yourself from the herd by wanting to add value to them in some sort of way.

Meeting My Mentor

Case in point: when I first got into the speaking world, I met Les Brown, one of my mentors, in San Diego for a speakers' training seminar he was putting on. I enjoyed myself and learned a great deal from him that day. I knew that I wanted to get to know him better and, what's more, be trained by him. But everyone around Les was all "take, take, take," asking for what they wanted instead of adding some value to his life.

So I stepped back to reconsider my skill sets and how they could possibly add value to the life of the great Les Brown. Well, I knew I had a marketing background and I thought I would offer to help with branding a new website and power voice program Les was implementing.

Through me offering my unique, voluntary and professional services, it created a symbiotic relationship that has grown into a true friendship and admiration to this day! Les is someone whose opinion I value and I look to him as a mentor and counselor for all areas of my business success.

Before and after each mentoring session with Les, I asked myself these questions to help me breakthrough:

- What would your DREAM Life look like?

- What would you be willing to do to accomplish your DREAM Life?
- What would you attempt if you knew you could not fail?

Well, for me, I have mentally put these questions to the test. In my mind, failure is not an option. I will do whatever it takes to be successful and to have the life my family deserves. When you ask yourself these questions, if you intend to be honest about the replies, you have to create a mindset shift, and mentally prepare to do whatever it takes to get you to your goal. Notice the word I used is "goal". That's because, to me, a goal is a dream written down.

Many people leave their dreams where they originate – in their heart or their head, and that's fine. But by committing them to paper, you can take action steps to accomplish them. This is a critical step to making your dreams a reality.

I believe that most people are basically good, kind and smart. They are talented, unique and their heads are filled with dreams. So why do so few people actually live their dream life? It's not because people are untalented, lazy or unwilling to work to achieve their dreams. I believe it's because they simply never make their dreams a reality by bringing them out of their heads.

Living the Dream Starts With Writing it Down: *What Does Your Dream Life Look Like?*

Dreaming is easy, but doing is hard; we all know that. But doing is not impossible and it starts with just that

– doing. You can't just dream it – or wish it so – and make it happen. You have to take that dream and give it life, which of course requires work.

One of the biggest enemies of dreams is our insistence that dreams just magically and suddenly "come true". That all we have to do is dream, win it big, strike rich and boom… there we go. But it's not the big events that make dreams a reality, but the daily, workaday routine that puts our feet on the ground and puts real muscle behind those dreams.

That's where goals come in. You write something down, you make it real. You give it life and you give it guardrails and parameters and due dates and deliverables.

So start writing down what you want. Make it very vivid and detailed, because the more you can actually see yourself accomplishing the dream – or goal – the more likely you are to do just that. Ask yourself, "What would my DREAM Life look like?"

As I stated earlier in the book, my dream life – or as I like to call it my future life – would look like this: I'm speaking to 60,000 people who paid to see me talk! I have been featured and interviewed by *Success* magazine. I have a million dollars – liquid – in my personal checking account. I have the number 1 bestselling book title in the New York *Times* and on Amazon.com. I have a private helicopter that takes me and my family in and out of the city from our private, obscure home in Northern California.

I'm able to send my wife on a shopping spree once a month in New York and Paris. I spend as much time with my kids as they want, without me worrying about the daily tug, pressures and grind of work. But enough about me, what *does* your Dream Life look like?

What Would You Be Willing to Do to Accomplish Your DREAM Life?

The last question I asked myself is probably the most important question of the group: What would you be willing to do to accomplish your DREAM Life? I always say most people will say they want to be rich or wealthy, but when push comes to shove they are simply not willing to do what it takes to be that.

For example, how many times over the course of December have you made a New Year's resolution to get healthy and start working out? Then New Year's Day comes around and you join the gym, buy all the cool looking workout gear, start reading the fitness magazines and maybe you even went out and bought a tread machine for the house.

You are ready to go!

The first day at the gym comes and you are excited about trying things you have never done before. You read the instruction on all the machines, so you can get the best workout for your money. You feel great and, even if you're a little sore, you go back the next day – and the next, and the day after that.

A few weeks go by and now the "noise" of your old life starts to set in. Your new resolution is wearing off, the working out is getting to be a grind and, after all, aren't there better things you could be doing with your time?

That's the "noise" I'm talking about: the mental distractions, the little voices inside your head that rob your dreams of becoming a reality: you need to put more time at the office, the kids need you to pick them up, I'm too sore,

I need to take a little break. Inevitably, the noise gets louder and louder and you start going less and less.

Now you're down to using the tread machine at home, because it's quicker and you can get back to your daily grind easier after you use it. Mind you, now, you are still paying for the gym membership, because you keep saying to yourself, "This is just temporary. I'm going to go back. Maybe tomorrow, just… let me step on this treadmill real quick and get a workout in first." Now weeks go by and you're using the tread machine less and less. Now it's basically an extra clothes rack in your room.

GAME OVER!

Habitual Behavior: *Your Secret Weapon of Mass Destruction*

You started out with great intentions but, the problem is, you were setting yourself up for failure all along. Let me explain: in what universe did you see yourself attempting to break your bad habits – or should I say, lack of good habits – all by yourself? Remember, your habits are what got you here in the first place. We all have habits, and those habits aren't "good" or "bad" in themselves. They are simply things that we have become accustomed to.

These habits, by and large, dictate our actions and, ultimately, our success – or failure. I read somewhere that it takes you doing something at least 21 times in order for it to become a habit. So if going into a gym by yourself, with no support, no coach and no life plan didn't become a habit, is it any surprise? Why did you think you could do it on your own, just by will power alone?

For me, the better approach would have been to partner with a friend or to get a trainer to hold you accountable, and make sure on the days you say you're going to work out for an hour that you actually do. This is applying goals, which are the building blocks of habitual behavior, into your life.

You set a goal – work out four days this week – and your spouse, your kids, your colleague at work, your mentor, your trainer can help you stick to that goal. The sooner you reach this goal, the closer you are to forming a habit; a lifetime habit.

Some of us do have the sheer willpower to do what it takes without mentors, coaches, trainers and the like, but most of us need help to stay on track and reach our goals.

By remembering to dream, writing those dreams down, turning our dreams into goals and, finally, getting help from someone like a mentor or a coach to help you create the habits needed to help you accomplish your goals, you too can create the solid habits of success. This is where you're willing to do whatever it takes to see your dreams or goals become a stone cold reality.

But it first starts with Dreaming Big…

Action Steps for Chapter 4

Before you get started using the lessons I've shared in Chapter 4, ask yourself these simple questions:

Am I feeling a little too comfortable in my life right now?

Does shaking things up scare me a little – or a lot?

Have I put limits on my dreams?

Do I recognize the power of mentors?

Is there someone I can approach to mastermind with?

Am I willing to give to my mentor so that it is a mutually beneficial relationship?

Chapter 5:
The Fourth Strategy – Reduce the Noise

"Self-discipline begins with the mastery of your thoughts. If you don't control what you think, you can't control what you do. Simply, self-discipline enables you to think first and act afterward."
- Napoleon Hill

Distraction or, as I like to call it, "noise," is the number one reason why most people don't get ahead. Now more than ever, distraction has been turned up to high volume. Thanks to technology, tablets, emails, texts, computers and smart phones we can literally be distracted in thousands of ways.

We can be distracted by:

- **A mobile application, or "app";**
- **A text requesting a conference call;**
- **A conference call;**
- **Ten texts setting up a conference call;**
- **A Skype call;**
- **An email;**
- **Ten emails about that last email;**
- **Ten texts on the way to a meeting;**
- **Thirty texts waiting for us the minute the meeting gets out;**
- **Etc.**

Many, many people fall prey to such distractions because, on the surface, they seem like important work. And, quite frankly, a lot of work is distracting because our bosses, our colleagues, our managers, our teammates, team leaders and even clients feel like if we're busy, we're working.

If you don't think distractions aren't part of the new, modern workplace, just try getting through a single day, technology (i.e. distraction) free. It is virtually impossible. Not just because so many companies use technology as part of the day to day grind, but because distractions are now part of the organizational culture of so many companies.

In fact, many companies reward their busiest, most "productive" employees despite the fact that their day is full of more distractions than there is actual productivity. In fact, many employees learn as early as business school that looking busy is almost good as *being* busy.

But not all work is created equal, and learning to tell the difference between distractions – or "noise" – and real progress is going to be a huge boost in reaching your Breakthrough moment in record time.

What Distractions (Really) Look Like

Think about it: have you ever been on a project with a very strict deadline and, the minute you sit down to finally start working, something always comes up? The phone rings, a text bleats, then another text, and you're late for a conference call, but there's that afternoon meeting and… before you know it, a whole day passes without a single moment of actual, forward motion productivity.

Let's say you're in sales and your job is to make calls. The only way you make your commission this month is by getting on the phone and starting to make those calls, one after the other. And before you begin, you know you're already behind the eight ball with your manager, so you need to hit this quota like never before. That's a major deadline, and a lot of stress, but you've done it before and you know, if you can just focus on hitting that quota, you can do it again.

So, you sit at your desk, completely focused on doing what needs to be done. I mean, you're fired up, in the zone, ready to conquer the world. The computer is on, you've got your list in hand, your phone is all charged up and ready to make calls and, all of a sudden, you look over at your "in" basket and notice this sheet of paper that has red ink all over it.

"Now, what is that?" you ask yourself, assuming it's something important. So, you pick it up, and suddenly you realize it was a bill you forgot to pay and, because it's critical to your success, now that becomes priority. You now take the remainder of the day working on your bills and never got to those calls. How is that productive? Who does that help? How will you reach your quota if, every day this month, you respond to the distractions – the noise – of our everyday world?

Or maybe you're an entrepreneur and you work from home and you know there are things you need to do to get your business on track. So, one morning you sit down and make a "to do" list of all thing things that MUST get completed that day! All of a sudden your beautiful wife comes in and says, "Hey, let's take a nap together." See, in our house, we have kids so "taking a nap" is our code word for, well… you get the point. It's a beautiful distraction, but still a distraction, and the enemy of productivity if you're an entrepreneur working from home.

As you can see, distractions come in all shapes and in all sizes. They can be your kids, TV, books, sales projections, bills, texts, tweets, social media, exercise, fitness, Netflix… just plain anything else other than your task at hand.

So, how do you cancel out distractions? How do you reduce the noise? For starters, you have to identify your distractions (see below). Next, you have got to become laser focused on what you want in order to achieve it. That means taking those distractions you've identified and either using them to your advantage or losing them altogether.

Identifying Your Distractions

If you've ever had to diet or get in shape, you know the power of identifying your problem foods or, in the case of physical fitness, your weaknesses. If you're a "carb addict," knowing this fact can give you the power to greatly reduce the amount of carbs you eat every day and, as a result, reach your Breakthrough weight goal. If you identify cardio as a weakness in your strength training plan, you can better focus your energies on running, jumping, swimming, climbing, etc., to turn this weakness into a strength.

Again, not all distractions are necessarily bad. We need some carbohydrates to function at capacity, and oftentimes poor cardio performance simply means we've been focusing on weight and strength training instead.

Likewise, our cell phones provide us with instant communication and, when used to broker deals, can make us big money. Our computers, tablets, laptops and other hard- and software technology can help us create amazing Breakthroughs we might not be able to achieve otherwise.

And yet, when abused, our technology can rob us of the precious, quality time we need to pursue our goals. Whiling away endless hours on the latest gaming app craze takes us away from what really matters, as do endlessly organizing and reorganizing the playlists we use to listen to while we work.

So the task at hand isn't necessarily to silence our cell phones or ditch our tablets or ignore our spouses when they want a little quality time, but to prioritize our goals and identify our distractions so that we're not robbing one by engaging in the other.

When I finally started working on becoming laser focused and attaining my own personal and professional Breakthrough, I asked myself these three simple questions:

1. *What would you accomplish without any distractions?*
2. *Name seven distractions that hold you back from having your Breakthrough? (i.e. cell phone, TV, technology, sports, family, etc.)*
3. *List the three distractions that take up most of your time?*

Answering these three questions will not only help you recognize the power of distractions, but more importantly will help you identify which distractions are holding you back from your ultimate Breakthrough:

The First Question: *What would you accomplish without any distractions?*

If you had no distractions in your life, what could you finally accomplish? Could you...

- Write a book?
- Go back to school?
- Take those acting classes like you said you were going to?
- Hit the gym two more days a week?
- Lose those extra fifteen pounds?
- Get that promotion you always wanted?
- Hit that rank that has eluded you for so many years?
- What could you do?

For me, because I work from home, I had to figure out the best time for me to work, the time that I would have the least amount of distractions so I could focus on my own Breakthrough.

This included, in great part, finding just the right time when my daughter Kahea wasn't demanding my time. You see, she is only five years old, so she doesn't understand work; she just wants to play with daddy. I also needed to figure out the time that my boys Chase and Chance don't need to be driven to some function, the time my wife Delilah doesn't want to take "naps," etc. (Smile).

In other words, I needed to find my optimal time slot.

For me, after much trial and error, I discovered that my ultimate, Distraction Free Zone begins at five in the morning. Think about it: no one else is up, there are no calls coming in, my daughter and wife are still sleep, the boys haven't even gotten out of bed yet for school, The only one that's up is my dog Max, who will sit by my desk and keep me company, all while saying nothing . This is my time; no distractions around to make the best of two full hours to accomplish the things that I must get done.

During this magical Distraction Free Zone time I wrote a book, I created a new workshop to teach my strategies, I launched two new marketing programs, I developed two clients' new brands and marketing campaigns. All during my optimal time slot, which gave me zero distractions.

So, what would *you* accomplish with no distraction? Let's find out: first off, find your own Distraction Free Zone. This is a time that not only works into your schedule, but allows you a solid two to three hours of uninterrupted productivity where you can really let loose and check off a variety of items on your "to do" list.

Every morning, from 5 AM to 7 AM, I have a set amount of goals – some big, some small – that I want to reach. It might be something like, "Reach 10,000-words in your new book" or "Finish formatting your website" or "Make five new business connections" or "Post two new training videos on YouTube," etc. Some days I might not complete all the tasks in my Distraction Free Zone, but that doesn't mean they won't get completed.

For instance, maybe I only got two videos shot, but not edited, in the morning between 5 and 7 AM, but I might finish editing them at night after the kids are asleep, and the next morning make posting them my first priority.

But either way, I know I get SO much more done without distractions than I do with them.

You need this in your life! I can't tell you how amazing it's been for me! To have a time just for you, which works into your schedule. Maybe this means you go into work earlier or stay later. Maybe its means you ask your boss to allow you to telecommute from home, if that is an option.

Find a way to be optimal, with as few distractions in your daily routine as possible. Once you find your optimal time slot, then prioritize your to-do list. Now, for me, my to-do list always includes income producing activities, not busy work. I can do busy work during the distraction hours. It doesn't require much thought or concentration to do busy work.

Once you have prioritized your list, pick the first thing and get laser focused on that action to accomplish that task. Only focus on that one thing, don't multi-task. Set your sites on that target, remember it's not Ready, Shoot Aim… It's Ready, Aim, Shoot. Stick with one thing, and stick with it until it is accomplished. Multi-tasking is a major distraction. By not focusing on a specific action step, you will find yourself not accomplishing your goal as fast as you could have if you were laser focused. Have your sites locked on your target, and get it done. That is the best way to utilize your Distraction Free Zone.

The Second Question: *Name seven distractions that hold you back from having your Breakthrough?*

Now that you've discovered the power of distractions – the power to unravel your goal setting

102

activities, that is – it's time to manage them. Notice I didn't say eradicate them. Distractions are a part of everyday life. From cell phones to text messages to your Netflix queue to your family, friends, holidays and celebrations, not all distractions are bad and sometimes… you just need to go on and watch a little TV or go to the movies!

Life can't just be work. We need distractions to help keep us sane and so in no way am I saying, "Kill your distractions!" But… we all know how easy it is for life's little distractions – even the "good" ones – to get in our way.

So for our next question, we need to get serious and list the seven distractions that most frequently keep us from productivity, from creation, from inspiration and, most importantly, that keep us from reaching our Breakthrough potential.

So, why seven distractions? Why not ten things that distract us? Or five? Or eight? Well, I'm just picking a number that is manageable to help you focus on your distractions and name them. Naming things – junk foods that make us fat, self-talk that defeats us, habits that weigh us down – helps us zero in on them so that we can fix them and improve ourselves.

So, here are some spaces and now I want you to fill them in with seven distractions that hold you back from having your Breakthrough:

1. _____
2. _____
3. _____
4. _____
5. _____

6. _____

7. _____

Now, remember, distractions can be literally anything: playing Xbox, constantly checking your social media accounts, family, friends, TV, movies, reading, music, going to concerts, eating out at restaurants, etc.

Be honest, be serious and list those seven distractions that you know, in your heart, are robbing you of your full Breakthrough potential. Next up, we are going to knock four items off your list:

The Third Question: *List the three distractions that take up most of your time?*

So, you've listed your seven biggest distractions. Congrats! Now I want to help you narrow that list down so that you can zero in entirely on those three distractions that take up the most of your time.

Are you an obsessive tweeter?

Do you constantly take selfies all day?

Are you taking longer and longer for lunch every afternoon?

Are you knocking off sooner and sooner every day to ride your new bike?

Remember, there are no "right" or "wrong" distractions, only those that you know are sucking the most time away from your most important dreams, habits, goals and desires; only those that are robbing you of your ultimate Breakthrough potential.

So, go ahead now, and from that original list of seven in the last question, whittle your list down to the three distractions that take up most of your time:

1. _____
2. _____
3. _____

Once you've identified your three biggest distractions, you can finally begin to do something about them. And you *must* do something about them, because only when you apply a laser-like focus to your efforts to Breakthrough, can you finally begin to achieve the results you've been looking for. And you simply can't do that when you're too easily distracted.

The Takeaway

As I said earlier, not all distractions are created equal and, frankly, not all distractions are bad. My wife Delilah uses distractions to her advantage by "toggling" between whatever presentation project she's working on. Whenever she needs to finish a presentation project, in order for her to work she must have the New Age radio station on, a number 2 pencil and blank pieces of paper, which allows her to take note swhile highlighting the section of the book she's reading. Then she writes down words to include in her power point, like a script on paper, then she proceeds to create the presentation.

Rather than the way I do it, which is in complete silence, with no noise at all. I start my presentation by looking up images on Google that I think will illustrate an emotion or feeling. I then place the images in power point to illustrate the story. Then I apply words that come to mind when I see the picture. Then I will research the word's meaning to make sure it applies to the meaning I'm trying to convey. Meanwhile, my wife is getting the same work done while listening to her New age music at the same time. While it might seem "distracting" to work that way to me, she can't really work any other way.

So it's not simply an issue of doing things one way, or even there being only one way. You have to find what works for you, which is why identifying your distractions are so mission critical to finding success.

And, just like every other factor in creating success, limiting distractions needs to be a habit, not an event. You can't just limit the amount of time you spend on social media – if that's your biggest distraction – one day and then, the next day, go right back to sending out 400 tweets, 200 selfies, 100 Facebook posts and 50 vine videos and expect to get anything done.

So identify your distractions, work to reduce them and keep working on reducing them every single day. That way you will get into the habit of avoiding distractions, rather than succumbing to them.

Action Steps for Chapter 5

Before you get started using the lessons I've shared in Chapter 5, ask yourself these simple questions:

Have I identified my major distraction(s)?

What am I willing to do to reduce this/these distraction(s)?

Is there something I can do to replace my distraction(s) with a positive habit (self-improvement, education, etc.)?

Have I notice any changes since I reduced the noise?

Chapter 6:
The Sixth Strategy – Strengthen Your "Why"

"He who has a why to live for can bear almost any how."
- Friedrich Nietzsche

I remember when I first got into direct sales, otherwise known as network marketing. I heard this guy say, "Your 'why' should be strong enough to move mountains." I didn't really understand what that meant until later, but it made me curious enough to dig just a little deeper with every prospect, candidate, connection or sale.

Eventually I realized that the more I knew about my "why" for selling the product, or joining a network, or marketing an incentive, the better I did – much better. It's called "the driving force," and it's the secret ingredient of sales success.

Understanding – And Obsessing Over – Your "Why"

So let's talk about *your* "Why" for a moment. Your why is your reason for doing, for being, for existing, for grinding it out, for toughing it out, for hustling all day and for humping it out.

Whatever you do, every time you do it, you need a why. We are human beings that are motivated by emotion, and it's those emotions that will focus us on accomplishing every task that we do. It's not enough just to understand your *reason* for doing something; you have to understand the emotion that compels you to do it in the first place!

I know this is a lot to swallow but, simply put, your "why" is the thing that gets you up in the morning, that makes you do the things you don't want to do, that makes you push yourself even when you've reached a certain level of success. Your why is that thing that helps you achieve that ultimate success when nothing else could.

When you find out what it is, I promise, that why will make you cry!

And that's the thing about why, really: once you figure out what your why is you will constantly think about it. From the time you get up in the morning to the time you go to bed, your why is with you every step of the way.

Now, almost everyone I talk to about their why confuses it with their passion. And I suppose it's quite natural, because passion is what fuels so much of our lives. But as you'll see in a moment, from my own personal story, passion is not enough to pull you out of a funk, get you over that farthest hill or up that highest mountain. Passion – what you're jazzed about right now, or maybe even were as a kid – only lasts so long, and when it's gone… where will you be?

Let me be quite clear: your why is different from understanding what you love to do, or even what you're passionate about. The cold, hard truth is that passion fades over time, but understanding what you're doing it for – or even who you're doing it for – will drive you harder, faster and longer than passion ever can.

I remember the first time someone asked me, "What's your why?" I immediately thought the person was asking me what I was most passionate about.

What is the one thing I would do even if I wasn't paid for it?

At the time, I thought consulting and running a huge business was what I loved to do. I mean, it's what I was jazzed about at the time, so... why wouldn't I be jazzed about it five, ten, twenty years from now? But as I got older, I realized that as human beings we are always evolving, growing and changing.

What excited me ten years ago, even five years ago, has changed, is changing and will keep changing. That passion that fueled my startup, my dream job, my own company, has altered and evolved, and so have I.

Now what am I supposed to do?

The things that I was passionate about when I started no longer motivated me to want that same job, position, company or career. But what was still in the back of my mind as I got up to go to work every day was why I was doing it in the first place. Or, in this case, who I was doing it *for*.

So that's your why. When all the dreams fade away and it's not about getting your dream job anymore, it comes down to what motivated you in the first place. What kept you going through all the crap and all the disappointments and all the challenges and the roadblocks to continue moving forward? Was it to protect your family? Was it to impress your friends? Was it to satisfy some inner desire for excellence, wealth or fame? We'll find out in a moment, but you have to dig deeper than just, "I've always wanted to do this" to get to your why.

I've talked to so, so, SO many successful people over the years and when you ask them what their why was, they all say it was an emotion inside of them that drove them every day to accomplish whatever goal they had in mind. Whatever they were successful in – real estate, Hollywood, music, fashion, modeling, extreme sports, entrepreneurism, technology – it was always bigger than just MONEY or the love of the game.

It wasn't always a positive thing. That's the big misconception about why, and another way in which it differs from passion. You follow your passion, it's always about what's good in your life. Sometimes, your why is about what's not so great in your life, and never going back there again.

For many of the successful people I've interviewed, in fact, their why often came down to the very simple, the very basic fear of losing. The fear that they wouldn't have what they desired most of all. See, it wasn't what they wanted so much, as being without it that drove them – and that's okay. Your why is your why, and that's okay, too. That negative emotion of fear of failure, of loss and of lack pushed them past all other obstacles to Breakthrough and achieve their results.

Just as many successful people cite someone, rather than some thing, as their why: their spouse, their mother or father, another family member and, quite often, their child or children.

The love of another motivated others to do more to accomplish their goals and desire so that they could provide for their spouse or child. That's a positive why that seems to be a polar opposite from passion, and which is why it's so important to make the distinction between the two.

Three Questions to Why

When I was at my lowest point in life, feeling miserable, like a failure, I somehow found the courage to ask myself these three questions to help me figure out my why:

1. *What is your why?*
2. *Will your why be strong enough to help you Breakthrough?*
3. *How often do you think about your why?*

In this next section, I want to run through these questions one by one, tell you how I answered them and then perhaps share a little about why each question is so vitally important to reaching your own personal Breakthrough:

Question # 1: *What is Your Why?*

As previously stated, your why is a difficult thing to explain. I've been trying to put into words how I feel, what my why is, but everyone's why will be different. Let me tell you a story that might help to explain: imagine you are deathly afraid of heights, but for some reason you are on top of a thirty-foot tall building and there is an equally tall building right across from it. A guy offers you a thousand dollars to walk across this piece of wood – which is about forty-feet long – from one building to the other.

Of course, being fearful of heights, you immediately say, "No!" (And even if you're not afraid of heights, you'd probably still say "No!") Now, picture the exact same scenario but the only difference is now the building across from you is on fire and, what's more, your child is over there, crying for you! What do you do? At this point, most people would walk across that wood plank and go save their child, no hesitation, no doubts, no ifs, ands or buts, even if it cost them their lives.

See, that was not passion; that was your why! Money didn't motivate you to look past your own fear, but the safety of your child made you do something that you would not normally – i.e. never – do! That is probably the best way I can explain it!

When determining your why, think of the one thing that would make you do something even if you didn't want to. See, most people would say money would make them do something even if they really didn't want to. Wasn't that the whole premise of the hit show, Fear Factor: You win money for eating bugs and jumping out of buildings and driving fast cars over cliffs?!? But I believe that money is not a strong enough why, because when you have the money then what do you do?

Most people I know would quit their jobs if they won the lottery. They are not working for their passion, they're not working for their why, they're just working for money. Do you think all those folks on Fear Factor would keep eating bug milkshakes if nobody was offering them thousands of dollars to do so? Money isn't enough to keep most of us going once we earn enough of it.

So what then? What's your why?

What about family? Maybe you're doing a job you hate or following a course that was set by someone else in your family. Maybe you've inherited the family business, or are working for your spouse's family business, or doing a job you know your spouse approves of but isn't necessarily your why.

You're doing what *they* want, not necessarily what *you* want. Eventually it will get old and you will realize that you're not happy and you're doing it for all the wrong reason, so that can't last. Family's out.

So what's left? What is your why? Where does it come from? How do you capture it, let alone follow it? Well, all I can say is figure out what is true for you. At the end of the day, it's something that will inspire you to do more, when more is needed. It could be something that scares you more than the task that's being asked of you, and stretch your comfort zone until it feels about ready to burst!

As in the example I used earlier in this chapter, you were more scared of the thought of losing your child than the fear of falling while walking across to that other building! Forget the fire, forget the drop, forget the fear… nothing was going to stop you from saving your child. Your why was staring you in the face and calling out your name.

As I shared with you earlier on in the book, my why is a memory that I never want to experience again, and because of that there is an extremely strong emotion attached to it! My why is powerful, focused, strong, vivid and there's not a day goes by that I don't reflect on those tough times and remember "why" I'm working so hard to avoid going back there. It may sound negative but, in fact, it creates a very positive environment of motivation, work ethic and satisfaction as I move forward each and every day.

You can't control your why, nor can you pick what it is. It's deep inside, it's emotional and it's uniquely your own. It can be a positive, or negative, emotion. Your why can be a passion you want to feel, a compulsion you have that you can't explain, something positive that gets you jazzed every day or, as it is for me, a dark place in your life you never want to revisit.

For me, my why is the one thing that motivates me every morning to get up and do what is needed to keep moving forward on my path of success. It is the thing I think about before I go to bed; it's the thing I think about when I wake up in the morning.

It's is always a constant reminder of how bad it could get and how vulnerable we all are to life's peaks and valleys, its ultimate highs and crashing lows. So as you start to ask yourself these questions, be honest with yourself. Take time to really search for your why; let it be something to help you move mountains.

What's your WHY?

Question # 2: *Will your why be strong enough to help you Breakthrough?*

Your why must be more than a simple shoulder shrug or pulse pounder, it must have stamina. That's why it's important to distinguish between your passion and your why.

Remember, to Breakthrough you have to change. You aren't breaking through now, or you wouldn't be reading this. I'm still breaking through, because I'm still changing. But I know why I want to Breakthrough, and that will guide what I will do – the actions I'll take – to Breakthrough.

Now, let me take you back to that rooftop once more. This time I want you to really, really picture it in your mind. Don't just picture it; feel it. Feel the wind in your face, the lump in your gut as you look down 30 stories to the cold, hard ground below. Realize that this isn't a video game, where you can just hit "replay" if you fall to the ground. Know that this is real life, gravity exists and if you fall, that's it… no more you.

In one scenario, I presented a pretty strong why: the building across the way was burning, and your child was screaming for help. Not many of us could resist the power, the pull, of that why.

But now let me throw out some alternate scenarios and see if they're strong enough to get you to walk over that 40-foot long two-by-four to the building across the way:

- **A big Hollywood producer is across the way, and offers you a four-picture deal in your favorite movie franchise, if only you'll take that 40-foot walk;**
- **Three bags of cash sit on that opposite roof, tax free, yours for the taking, if only you'll take the risk;**
- **Donald Trump is over there, offering you a job running one of his many properties, and a prime position in his company, and all you have to do is take that first step;**

- **The president is standing there, hand out, to welcome you to his Cabinet, and all you have to do is ask – oh, and walk across that 40-foot plank.**
- **Your boss is standing over there, offering you his job, and all you have to do is take it from him…**

As you can see, very few of these offers can motivate you the way fear, joy, happiness or hope can. We'll do almost anything for money, but not everything, and if money is our only why, well… it's never quite enough. Jobs, positions, authority, security, even fame and power are never quite strong enough to fuel us past the initial desire to be rich, famous… or both.

This exercise should help you see that it takes more than just money, power, prestige or even desire to get you to go through the hard work, effort and change required to really Breakthrough. You will need to dig deep and discover a why that goes beyond the surface and cuts deep to what it is that really drives you.

Think about why you bought this book. Was it just to make more money? Be more successful? I sincerely doubt it, because nowhere in this book's title, subtitle or even its Introduction or back copy does it say: earn more money with this book. Or be more successful, or prettier or more popular, or more powerful.

Breaking through is about reaching your highest potential. That could mean graduating college, getting your Master's Degree or Ph.D., getting your first job, your first promotion, your first leadership role, your first company, your first franchise or hitting the highest rank in your network marking company. Whatever you want to achieve, no matter how big or how small, you need a Breakthrough to do it. Understanding why you want to Breakthrough will actually help you achieve that goal.

Let's say your quest is not for money or fame, but for educational excellence. You live for books, for classes, for achieving the next highest goal in education after the one you've currently set your sights on. Why? Why do you strive so hard to write your doctoral dissertation or study for your oral exams? Why is it so important to intern for this prestigious foundation, and teach summer classes at this Ivy League school? Why do you care if this educational publisher puts out your new book, or that one does?

Look closely at your life. What is your why? Examine it, peel back the layers. Perhaps, when you were growing up, you were the first one in your family to get a formal education, perhaps even the first to graduate high school. As such, your family instilled in you a deep and abiding respect for higher learning that goes well beyond money, fame or even prestige.

Your why is making your family proud in the lifelong pursuit of educational excellence. That desire is so strong it propels you even when your eyes ache from studying or your neck's sore from behind hunched over a laptop all morning. That is a lifelong why, a why so deep it's woven into your DNA and simply won't let you stop until you are personally and professionally satisfied.

And that why will be strong enough, I believe, to help you Breakthrough any educational, emotional, spiritual, personal and professional challenges you face along the way.

So, is *your* why strong enough? Will it be enough to fuel your Breakthrough? Read on to find out:

Question # 3: *How often do you think about your why?*

How much is too much when it comes to thinking about your why? Is enough ever enough? Can you ever think about your why *too* much? I like to say that my why is like a constant running stream, just below the surface. Every day I wake up and listen to it gurgle, a little louder than during the more hectic and active parts of my day, and then in the quiet times it is still there, bubbling up again, and always at night, before I go to bed, I'm thinking about my why, what makes me special, what drives me forward and how I can go even farther the next day.

I guess what I mean to say, you will think of your why more often in times of need, and less often in times of right. For instance, there are times in my career where I am in growth mode, but not necessarily rapid growth mode. I think we both know what I mean by that.

In other words, in good times I can't exactly coast along, but at least the days aren't filled with as much intensity and drama as, say, when I'm starting up a new company, facing a crisis, creating a new program or workshop, etc. So when things are in a certain gear, I may not think of my why quite so often, but when I'm feeling anxious or excited about a challenge or an opportunity, I may think about my why constantly throughout the day!

So, how often will you think about your why? That will depend, naturally, on what you're going through at the moment. While reading something like this, where you're hopefully getting informed, educated and inspired about your why, you shouldn't stop thinking about it!

The Takeaway

At the end of the day, no one but you can determine your why. But you must, and here's why: without a reason to go on, without a burning why inside of you, it gets harder and harder to push through the mundane, the routine, the ordinary and reach your ultimate Breakthrough moment.

Your why will propel you, through good times and bad, to succeed even when life has you beaten down. When I lost everything – twice – I had to reach down and rediscover my why so that I could draw upon that inner strength to do those things I needed to do, even though I feared I might fail again.

Think of your why like an extra gas tank hidden in your trunk, there for when you need it the most – especially when you break down on the side of the road, with no help in sight. You may become preoccupied with the "other stuff" of your days: the work routine, the grind, the deadlines, the "to do" lists, but never forget your why. Because when things fall apart or opportunity presents itself, you will need your why to rise above the routine, find another gear and reach that optimal strength you need to Breakthrough and move on to the next level.

Action Steps for Chapter 6

Before you get started using the lessons I've shared in Chapter 6, ask yourself these simple questions:

Do I appreciate the power of my why?

Do I understand the distinction between passion and my why?

Do I know what my "why" is?

Do I feel different now that I understand and recognize my own personal why?

Chapter 7:
The Sixth Strategy – Become a Better U

"When you become better, it enriches everything in life. The way you love, care or handle problems, seems easier because you're better."
- Cory J. Chapman

As we wind down to finally reach our sixth strategy, I want to spend some time discussing how to Become a Better U. I firmly believe that growth is a natural human state, that if we're not growing we're dying and that human nature is to always seek a higher vantage point, even if we're already standing on a mountaintop.

America, in particular, thrives on a culture of self-improvement. Whether we're actively doing so or not, nearly everyone we know is continually, energetically working on making themselves better. From diet books and gym memberships to seminars with self-help gurus, talk shows, MBAs and more, we are a country of dreamers, of doers, and of self-improvers.

So, how do I become better? It's a question I ask myself nearly every day, starting when I woke up at 4:30 in the morning that fateful day, wondering to myself, "How do I become better?"

See, I wasn't asking God to make my life easier that day, but for Him to grant me the wisdom to be better at handling my problems. Everyone has problems, they're inescapable, but it's how you handle those problems that will ultimately shape your future.

Many of us crumble when problems arise. We spend so much of our life carefully crafting a world with shock protectors, with high walls, with carefully constructed barriers, all to keep trouble away. When we miss a deadline, when a contractor fails to deliver, when supplies run out, when a typo costs us that big deal, when we blow a giant interview… we're lost, incapable of accepting defeat, or managing crisis.

But life is about choices, and if we can't avoid problems, if trouble eventually finds us, if challenges are often in our way, we must choose to do something about it, or suffer the consequences.

Remember, every **action** has a **reaction**:

- If I don't pay my light bill (*action*) they cut off the power (*reaction*).
- If I don't finish this paperwork on time (*action*), my team won't reach its deadline (*reaction*).
- If I don't take this last class (*action*), I won't get my graduate degree (*reaction*).
- If I don't pay my credit card bill (*action*), they eventually cut off my line of credit (*reaction*).
- If I don't show up for that interview (*action*), they won't consider me for the job (*reaction*).
- If I don't **fill in the blank** (*action*), they will **fill in the blank** (*reaction*).

In short, everything we do shapes our future. And I do mean everything, from the big to the small and everything in between. From the people we hang out with, to the stories we tell ourselves, to the books we read or don't read, the things we do or don't do, the habits we create, ignore or deny.

Are You Letting Life Happen TO You? Or Making it Work FOR You?

Our life is a composite of everything that's ever happened to us. When we ignore that fact, when we discount the daily little influences that shape who we are, how we live and who we'll become, we let life happen *to* us rather than make life work *for* us.

The two may sound similar but, in fact, are quite different. When life happens to us, we are a passenger on our own journey, going wherever life takes us with little to no control. When we make life work *for* us, however, we are in the driver's seat, shifting the gears, following the path we know we must take.

Here are some simple questions to ask to see if you're letting life happen to you, or making life work for you:

- **Do I feel in control of my life?**
- **Am I at the mercy of the decisions of others?**
- **Do I work for myself?**
- **Do I *feel* like I work for myself?**
- **Do I make plans – or excuses?**
- **Do I work independently?**
- **Do I feel confident in my own abilities?**
- **Does my team dictate my own performance?**

The fact is, we all hand over the wheel from time to time. Life is full of interior and exterior forces, some that we can control, some that we can't. I was making one heck of a living, working hard, when the real estate bubble burst.

That aspect of the situation was completely, irrevocably and totally out of my hands. I could not control the housing market, the fear my clients were feeling, the price of homes or even the fate of my employees as housing prices fell and fell and kept on falling.

That exterior factor meant that, however temporarily, life was happening to me. It continued to happen to me as I struggled through the loss, fear, anxiety and, ultimately, depression in the months, even years, that followed.

My life grew dark, bleak and hopeless. That is, until I finally decided to unfasten my seatbelt, get out of the passenger seat, slip back behind the wheel, grip it tightly, take my foot off the brake and apply some gas to get my life back on track.

It wasn't easy, and it didn't happen overnight, because shifting gears is a gradual process, not a one-time event. But if I hadn't started to make life happen for me – through purposeful, powerful and passionate action – I'd still be sitting in the passenger seat, letting life happen to me.

So, what gear are you in?

We Are Who We Surround Ourselves With

We often think that becoming better is all up to us, but the fact is if we hang around with the wrong people, they are helping to take that control away from us. And if we hang around with the right people, they are actively helping us achieve a level of "better" that we might not

125

have been able to reach without their assistance, guidance or mentorship.

People matter, more than you think. It's easy to think that we exist on an island, in and of ourselves, but everyone we come in contact with – our family, our friends, our neighbors, our coworkers, the guys on our softball team, the girls in our book club, managers, supervisors, teammates, classmates, leaders, CEOs – they all contribute to who we actually are.

People are like energy, and whether we know it or not, whether we're conscious of it or not, that energy infects us. Hang around with positive people, and you will get infected by their energy, their enthusiasm, their creativity, passion and positivity. Hang around with negative people, and the same infection will occur, only this time it will flood your system with bad vibes, negative thoughts, doom and gloom.

If you don't believe me, just begin to quietly observe the groups where you work. Notice how negative, doom and gloomers tend to cluster together, moaning and groaning and complaining. You'll never see a positive person hanging out with them. And even if you do, they won't stay long. Why? Because they won't be able to stand the constant stream of negativity with which they're surrounded all day long.

Now watch the positive people: they tend to be with other positive people. They laugh, they smile, they plan, they do, they problem solve, they console, they comfort, because they infect each other with their enthusiasm, positivity and optimism.

Energy feeds off energy. Positive energy feeds off positivity, while negative energy feeds on negativity. You can't fuel negativity with positivity, it's like putting wiper fluid in the gas tank – one of these things is not like the other. Energy is attracted to like forms of energy.

Why do you think creative types – actors, musicians, singers, dancers, writers, producers, choreographers, directors, conductors – always tend to cluster around each other, in New York or LA or Chicago or Atlanta or South Beach? It's because they are naturally attracted to that creative energy that gives fuel to their inspiration, their art and their passion.

We all tend to do this, in our own lives. We look for people with similar interests as ours, similar mentalities, personality, energy and enthusiasm levels. We form leagues and teams and book clubs and mommy play dates and study groups and think tanks with those who not only think, act and talk like us, but who help improve the way we think, act and talk.

Likewise, when we do tend to dwell in those places where we don't fit, or no longer fit as in the case of old friends or family members, the effect is both immediate and toxic. Like a nerve gas, every word of negativity, selfishness, pessimism and gloom saps our energy, our strength and, worst of all, our momentum.

But often, we don't know any better, we are afraid of offending, or have always had this toxic person in our life, and it not only affects us but invites us to be just as toxic: to them, to ourselves and to everyone around us. We can easily slip into negativity and toxicity if we're not careful, particularly when for whatever reason we either choose to hang around toxic people, or are too afraid to confront them or drop them from our lives.

Case in point: Have you ever found yourself in a conversation that you knew was toxic, one you knew you shouldn't be listening to, let alone contributing your input, and yet you continued anyway? Why? Why do we allow toxic, negative, even harmful people access to our lives, let alone our conversations, interactions, hopes, dreams, plans and outcomes? Why do we spend time on conversations that do nothing, say nothing and, worst of all, add nothing to our lives?

We like to call this gossip, and occasionally it's fun. There just seems to be something about talking about someone else's misery that makes our lives seem that much better. Compared to what they're going through, our lives don't seem so bad. It's kind of a, "Well, at least I'm not that guy" feeling, but do we ever stop to think about what "that guy" is going through?

Gossip websites and tabloids and the TV news cycle are full of stories of other people's misery, and it all seems so far removed from our own lives that we can hardly relate to this celebrity's divorce, or that NBA star's legal troubles. Even in our close circles, the whole "Did you hear about Harry and his wife?" mentality seems to be the norm rather than the exception. But every time we dip into that pool of gossip and hearsay, we cheapen ourselves just a little, and rob ourselves of the positivity and momentum that propels us toward our Breakthrough.

We can control our futures by controlling who we choose to surround ourselves with. I believe that firmly. Think about it: have you ever realized that the people you hang out with play a significant role in your success – or failure? I like to say if you're the smartest, wittiest or most successful person in your circle of friends, then it's time for

128

a new circle because there's nowhere to go from there. You simply can't grow if you have nothing to aspire to, and no one to mentor your growth to the next level.

Have you ever heard the saying, "You can't miss what you never had"? When it comes to who you hang out with, I take this to mean that if you never reach beyond your same circle, talking about the same things, in the same way, over and over again, you'll never know what might be just around the corner, with another group of friends.

Instead of talking about who's getting divorced or who's sleeping with who or last night's sports scores or what school teacher is quitting, you could be talking about:

- **New ideas;**
- **Investment strategies;**
- **Local opportunities;**
- **Entrepreneurial endeavors;**
- **Philanthropic causes;**
- **New technology;**
- **Self improvement;**
- **Etc.**

But like I said earlier, you can't miss what you never had. If you never even imagine that people talk like this, how will you ever know to go looking for them?

I made a comment some chapters back about only working on income generating ideas in my prime time zone of opportunity from five to seven a.m. every morning. That means my focus is solely on income, opportunity, growth and potential. I'm not doing busy work or paperwork or anything unless it has the potential to grow my earnings.

Frankly, I think of my free time in much the same way. While I'm not obsessed over money, I do consider my time valuable and I can't stand to waste it blathering about things that don't improve my life. I'm not talking just monetarily. I can gain value from reading a good book, listening to a wise friend – or simply someone with more experience than me in an area I'm interested in – school me on this, that or the other.

My friends, family, colleagues, peers and mentors excite and inspire me – and I hope that I, in turn, inspire them – because we all aspire to greater heights, want to better ourselves, earn more, be smarter, be better… Breakthrough. I value not only the time I spend with people, but the people I spend time with. I want to spend my time with "rich" people, not just rich in money but rich in ideas, in empathy, in inspiration, creativity, generosity and compassion.

I don't want to spend my time with "cheap" people. Again, I'm not talking about people who don't have money, but who cheapen my time and theirs by talking about nonsense or actively bringing me down with their negativity, doom and gloom.

That's why I always make it a point to surround myself with successful, inspiring, caring individuals with the same likeminded belief in bettering themselves that I have. We constantly push each other for greatness and not just in a random, event-like atmosphere once a quarter. This is regular, habitual and supportive behavior that we share with one another all year long.

In fact, we have a weekly mindset group call, one that is designed to talk about whatever challenges we are facing, what road blocks may be in our way, what solutions

130

we may have found and, finally, we explore new goals and ideas we may have for each other, our enterprises and the coming week.

We network our relationships to help each other reach a higher level of success. Imagine a group of like-minded people who support you, encourage you, engage you, push you, test you and inspire you to reach your ultimate Breakthrough. That's what I mean by being with "rich" people, folks who may not be billionaires, but who add value to your life rather than chip away at your confidence, resolve, ideas and opportunities.

Three Hour, Thirty Minute and Three Minute Friends

It sucks to have folks constantly pulling you down, or away from your goals, or telling you that you'll "never do this" or "never do that". After awhile, despite your best intentions, you begin to believe them. But with your own mindset group, you can avoid all that. You can turn free time, time that you would have spent just sitting around chewing the fat, into quality time that builds strength, encourages growth and adds value to your life and ideas.

So, what type of friends do *you* hang out with? Be honest because, honestly, unless they are fellow mindset builders they're probably never going to read this. I like to classify friends – pretty much everyone, really – in one of three categories:

1. **Three Hour Friends;**
2. **Thirty Minute Friends;**
3. **Three Minute Friends.**

If you think you know where I'm going with this, good, but you may be surprised. Why? Here, let me explain:

Three Hour Friends

Look closely at your friends (to include your colleagues, neighbors or anyone you spend a great deal of time with): Are they the type of friend that you could spend three hours sharing ideas with, collaborating on projects and generally adding value to each other's lives?

Are you sorry when you see them go, because you've come to associate their faces, their voices, their attitudes and expressions as a positive thing, something you know you're going to miss the minute they leave the room?

That's a three-hour friend, someone who enriches your life, adds value to it and makes you eager to see them again. When looking to make new friends, or ditch your old ones, always be on the lookout for a three hour friend.

Thirty Minute Friends

Or do you have friends that you would only want to spend thirty minutes with, because the minute you're together they immediately – and constantly – tell you their problems? Rather than focus on the positive, these folks have a tendency to share all of the bad stuff that's going on in their life, always with the "woe is me" mentality.

And forget ever asking anything about you. These are friends in name only. Maybe you grew up with them and they've always been like this, but you didn't really notice until you actually started thinking about what kind of friend they really were.

Maybe they were a former roommate who, ten years later, you can't believe you ever slept in the same room with. Or maybe they're a new friend, and because you have manners it's basically hard to get rid of them. And, frankly, the only reason they're thirty minute friends is because it takes so long to *get* rid of them!

Regardless of how you know them, these are some of the most toxic folks around. Unlike your three hour friends, who you can't wait to see coming, thirty minute friends constantly rob tiny little chunks of your life. Thirty minutes here, a half-hour there, time you'll never get back and that is cheapened by their selfish, petty, doom and gloom ramblings.

But as bad as thirty minute friends are, they're nothing compared to our last category:

Three Minute Friends

Finally, are your "friends" three-minute friends that, the minute you see them coming, you try everything possible to get away from them? That's because you know they are toxic, you know they cheapen your time together and that they are going to suck the life out of you every time they call or darken your doorstep. You look at the number on your cell and know you shouldn't answer but, for some reason, you do.

That's the thing about friends: whether out of loyalty or guilt or commitment or simply for "old time's sake," we feel compelled to stay friends with them. When they are three hour friends, that's not so very hard to do. But when

133

they venture into thirty minute or three minute friend territory, however, look out!

Lose the Dead Weight: *Your Breakthrough Depends On It*

When it comes to friends, colleagues and acquaintances, you should always – and I do mean always – surround yourself with people that add value to your life while equally striving to add value to their lives as well. In order to have a great, long lasting relationship, it should be mutually beneficial to both parties.

But what about when the relationship *isn't* so great? What about those thirty and three minute friends who drag you down, waste your time and drain you of your energy and momentum, like so many "time vampires"? Right about now, or perhaps even all through that last section, you are probably thinking of someone – or several someone's – who add no value to your life and, in fact, worsen it with their negativity, hostility and pessimism.

I am giving you permission to drop those people, to lose them from your life. You have to save yourself, and while your very life may not depend on it, your Breakthrough certainly does. It is extremely difficult to be your best self if you are surrounded by folks who are constantly frittering away at your self-confidence.

Life is full of decisions, some of them harder than others. Remember earlier when I talked about action, reaction and the choices we make that ripple through our lives? This is one of those choices you must make, hard as it is: to keep enduring a friend who really isn't good for you, or to take steps to remove that person from your day-to-day life.

Think of how often you talk to those thirty or even three minute friends: a day, a week, a month, a year! It can really add up! Isn't that time you could be spending improving yourself instead? Or spending with mindset mentors who can help you learn, grow and Breakthrough?

Time is precious, particularly when you're trying to better yourself. If I sound overly passionate about this topic it's because I value my time so strongly that I simply refuse to waste it on "time vampires" anymore, and you should, too. So, what to do? In the next section I'll provide you with a handy field guide to the Nine Personalities That Will Rob You of Your Breakthrough:

Nine Personalities That Will Rob You of Your Breakthrough

The following list is by no means complete. I'm sure you could add to it with a personality or two that you know quite well (and feel free to do so!). But these are the nine types of personalities I have personally witnessed rob people, not only myself, of their potential Breakthrough:

1. **The Chatty Cathy:** This person isn't really negative, or positive, or rich, or cheap, or optimistic, or pessimistic. They're not really anything at all other than loud, talkative and aggressively annoying. But their incessant talking about virtually nothing at all takes time away from the vital conversations, or simply just contemplative silence, that we all need to better ourselves.
2. **The Nervous Nelly:** Like yawning, anxiety can be catchy. So I generally avoid nervous, anxious people

in my life because they tend to infect me with their anxiety. What's more, nervous people tend to "qualify" everything. Things may be going great, "but" there is always a storm looming on the horizon. I know from storms, and I know from sunlight, and I prefer to enjoy the sunlight until the storm comes, not sit around waiting for the rain to fall.

3. **The Passive Aggressive:** There is almost nothing worse than somebody who smiles while stabbing you in the back, cutting you down, insulting you, talking about you behind your back, running you down or generally just robbing you of your time. They will play the nice guy, and are so good at confrontation that if you do say something to them about their behavior, they often have the canny ability to turn it around so you feel like the guilty party! Avoid these folks like the plague!

4. **The Angry Andy:** Angry people infect your life with anger as well. They inject that anger into every meeting, greeting, occasion, event and confrontation, which they enjoy. The trouble with angry people is that they're really not happy – i.e. don't get a "payoff" – until everyone around them is unhappy as well. Don't fall for it. "Kill them with kindness," as my better half says!

5. **The Time Vampire:** Time vampires make pretty lousy friends, because they suck and suck and suck little bits and pieces of your time until you look up and, wow… half the day is wasted! They're good about not taking up too much of your time, but only robbing you of a piece here and a piece there. Every

meaningless conversation, inane request, bit of gossip or confession just derails you from whatever it is you were doing.

6. **The Drama Queen:** Drama Queens – and Kings, let's not forget the guys here – are always, always, always in the middle of a crisis. Nothing is ever on time, nothing ever goes as planned, no shipment ever arrives in full, no order is ever perfectly right. Their biggest payoff is from the adrenaline rush they feel every time there is another "emergency," which to the rest of us just looks silly, of course. True drama happens to us all, but (hopefully) not every day!

7. **The Dream Killer:** While all of the folks on this list are "bad" for bettering yourself in some way or another, I want to say that Dream Killers are actually the worst. Why do I say that? Because dreams are precious, and too few people have them – let alone ever achieve them. So anyone who kills dreams is on my "cross off the list" list. You know the type: if you say you're going to try this, they'll make a face – you know that face – and say, "Hmm, you might want to aim a little lower." Or, "Are you sure you're up for that?" Or, "It's not really the best time for that right now." What they're really saying, of course, is: that dream will never come true, so why even bother? I believe that every dream is worth pursuing. Get out of my way if you don't agree!

8. **The Trouble Borrower:** People who "borrow trouble" are perhaps one of my least favorite types of people. You know the type: everything can be going well, but this person will always point out the one, two or two dozen ways in which things could go

horribly wrong. They are only happy when they're worrying, and like angry people they are happiest when everyone around them is worrying, too. Trouble will find us all at some point or another, but I prefer to not go looking for it, thanks very much.

9. **The Know It All:** This is the person that constantly thinks they know everything. They are the ones who will correct you on every mistake. They will be the first one to point something out and give their opinion, even when you didn't ask for it. They have no filter when it comes to their inflated ego and their sense of knowing all. I believe that you should only offer your opinion when asked, not volunteer simply for the sake of hearing yourself speak.

I know it's never easy to cut someone off completely, so don't. Just make it clear, starting now – even if it's only to yourself – that you're not going to allow these people to rob you of your Breakthrough. Then take active steps – avoiding their calls, not returning their texts, confronting them directly – to gently, gradually, gracefully and tactfully remove them from your lives.

It's not a sin to take care of yourself, and you're not responsible for the behavior of others. All you can do is control how you live your life, and that includes how you spend your time and, in this case, who you spend it with.

And aren't you worth it?

Knowledge is Power

Just as important as surrounding yourself with positive people who feed your soul, feeding your mind with knowledge is paramount to becoming a better person and reaching your ultimate Breakthrough.

I am a firm believer that you must constantly be growing. If you're not growing, I believe, you're dying. Sounds extreme, I suppose, but think about it: what's the point if all you're going to do is stay right where you are? We're not built that way, the human race. We're built to move, to explore, to try, to do, to achieve and then try and achieve some more.

The power to do more comes from knowing more. That's right: knowledge *is* power. That is, knowledge is power **when action is taken**. You can't just know something; you have to act on it for that knowledge to be vital and powerful.

I read an article awhile back that said most people never pick up a book (for learning) after leaving school. Imagine never picking up another educational tool once your education is completed.

That is so the opposite of how I live, or how the people I surround myself with live as well. I believe, we believe, that your education is never complete. Even dying is an education. The "last" lesson, if you will, but there are so many more, I hope, before we reach the final "classroom" of our lives.

Because I know the power it provides, because I know how it gives me the very tools I need to grow and improve myself, I have become a person who is thirsty for knowledge. I crave it like an addict and get my "fix" any way I can: in books and on audio, in person and online, any way and every way I can obtain knowledge, I will and I do.

And frankly, nowadays, there is no excuse for not seeking out a little bit of knowledge every day. Once upon a time we had to wait for knowledge. Wait for the library to open, to get to school, for our professor's office hours, for the semester to start, for the book we ordered to come in.

Nowadays, knowledge is literally instant. It has become so much easier to get the knowledge we need to better ourselves, Breakthrough and succeed in life. I mean we have the internet, audio books, lectures, smart phones that can play your favorite poem, books that can be downloaded to your tablet, speeches and seminars and lesson plans that can be viewed on your phone.

There have been times when I'm on a conference call or mindset call and someone I respect mentions a book or even just an author in passing and, while I'm on the phone, I can look it up, buy it for my iPad and begin reading it the minute I hang up. If I'm stuck in traffic I can call up my YouTube account on my phone and watch or listen to one of my favorite podcasts, lessons or sermons. I can have my iPad read to me when I'm too busy to turn the pages. I don't have to wait for that new bestseller to arrive, I can order it instantly. I can take classes online and receive knowledge I never dreamed of, with nothing more than a few mouse clicks.

All I'm saying is, if there was ever a time to become better through knowledge, it would be now. All you have to do is take the first step, and decide to do something.

The Takeaway

Never, ever, EVER stop trying to get better. Even if all you do, every day, is just a little thing, it's better than nothing. An inspirational quote, listening to a book on tape, talking to a mindset mentor, trying something new, bookmarking a new website, finding a useful way to organize or categorize, jotting down a new idea – these are all random, but excellent, examples of the many ways we can be improving ourselves every single day.

Action Steps for Chapter 7

Before you get started using the lessons I've shared in Chapter 7, ask yourself these simple questions:

Describe the type of people you spend the majority of your time with. (i.e. positive, negative, supportive, dream stealers, gossipers, worker bees, entrepreneurs, etc.)

How do these people add value to your life?

Are you willing to do something about them (i.e. drop them) if they don't?

What do you say when you talk to yourself?

List three words that describe you.

What do you see when you look at yourself in the mirror?

Would others see the same thing?

Once you become a better you and have your "Breakthrough," what does your life look like?

Chapter 8:
The Seventh Strategy – All Out Massive Action (A.O.M.A.)

"The path to success is to take massive, determined action."
-Tony Robbins

Okay, so we've learned what a Breakthrough is and even how to achieve one, but it doesn't just happen all by itself, so now it's time to go to work. It's time to put your foot on the pedal and go as fast as you can. Put your head down and drive. See, before now you thought it was okay to take your time and go slow on your dreams.

You said over and over to yourself:

- *"I have time, it will still be there."*
- *"Let me just take care of this first."*
- *"Well, this came up, let me run here now."*
- *"I've still got time to do this."*
- *"If I can just get this done over here, I'll get to that..."*
- *"Someday I will accomplish my dreams."*

I know it so well because I was that guy. I put everything off until someday. Well, guys, today *is* that someday. You can't wait for another one, because you have to act like today is all we've got. What I have learned hanging out with successful people is they go fast.

They don't wait until tomorrow to do what can be done today. They want it now – right now – and they are willing to put in something they call All Out Massive Action (A.O.M.A.) to achieve it.

Life at the Speed of Inspiration: *All Out Massive Action (A.O.M.A.)*

Life takes time, and while we're taking our time, other things happen to our dreams. If we don't seize opportunities as they come or, better yet, make them without waiting for them to come, we keep our dreams in place and achieve them much, much faster.

I appreciate the wisdom life has given me, some of it from age, some of it from experience, some of it from life's hard knocks. But I learn fast and life comes faster and that's what successful people know that, perhaps, the rest of us don't: life moves fast, and success moves even faster.

Let me tell you, if you ever had success at anything, it's so much better when you achieve that success fast then going through the painstakingly slow process of achieving it over years and years.

Case in point: when I was in network marketing I remember someone told me to join this company and use the first 30 days and "go all out"! He told me to think of myself like a rocket, explaining the analogy this way: a rocket uses more than 70% of its fuel just to break out of the earth's gravity. I thought that was kind of an interesting concept, and decided to take that new piece of inspiration and really do something special with it.

So, using that rather unconventional advice, over the next 30 days we took a $1,000 investment and turned it into a $15,000 return, while helping six other people qualify for a new BMW, and twelve other people receive a passive part-time income.

I remember that, during the same time period (30 days), there were people who decided to go slow and get through their network over the next six months and had no real success to speak of, and were even having thoughts of quitting. But, because of going all out for thirty straight days, we achieved far greater success than I had ever imagined. I never forgot that lesson, and use it to this day to fuel my dreams, desires and, ultimately, my Breakthrough.

There comes a time in your life that you have to think not with deliberation or doubt, but with a brisk sense of urgency. It takes confidence to think this way, and even more confidence to act, but I believe if you follow these seven steps that confidence will come naturally.

Why so speedy? I believe that life teaches us hard lessons and one of them is that, quite honestly, tomorrow may never come. I'm at an age now where I have had friends, good friends, pass away far too young, but that's far from uncommon. I'm looking at my parents and my wife's parents and appreciating how they make the best of every day because they learned that lesson long ago.

I believe it is our duty to live life full out, and that anything else wastes the good talents God gave us. I believe you're here, too, because you're looking to accelerate your current pace of success. We both are; that's why I wrote a book called Breakthrough and you're reading it! Think about that word for a minute: Breakthrough. Doesn't that just scream acceleration? Drive? Speed?

That's what this section is all about: speed, power, persistence, drive, never quitting and always, always, always doing whatever it takes, as fast as you can, to go after your dream.

A lot of people play by the rules and expect success to come in time, but the successful people I follow preach the power of speed and the fuel that massive, all out action provides. If you want to wait, wait, but don't expect that ultimate Breakthrough you've been working toward. We talked earlier in this book about wanting something different even while doing the same thing, and just how absolutely crazy that is.

If you want your Breakthrough, and you want it now, you have to act on your dreams, your goals, your vision and your why. But not just act, you have to massively act, all out, with the quickness. You have to feel a sense of urgency, you have to believe that this opportunity may never come again.

Here is what I want for you:

- **I want you to be excited about your Breakthrough.**
- **I want you to be in love with reaching your goals.**
- **I want you to go all out, all in, every single day.**
- **I want you to drop into bed, exhausted, from chasing your dreams.**
- **I want you to wake up, every morning, tired in a good way, energized by what might happen.**
- **And above all, I want you to stop coasting through life…**

What do I know about coasting? More than you'd think:

Life Starts When You Stop Coasting

I woke up one morning recently and asked myself:

- *What's been stopping me lately?*
- *Where did this wall come from?*
- *Why am I not seeing more success in my life, despite how hard I work?*
- *What did I do differently, if anything, when I **was** having success?*
- *How do I duplicate that process, again and again and again, so I can stop hitting these same roadblocks every few months/years?*

I had reached a plateau of sorts, a kind of middle ground where things weren't really bad but, then again, they weren't all that great, either. And still, I was bothered, perplexed, frustrated. I was sick and tired of being sick and tired. I was tired of the ups and downs, the fits and starts, the sprints and the setbacks. I wanted to keep some stability in our life. I wanted to stop having these major highs followed by these major lows. *What is it that I'm missing?* I wondered *Why do I keep repeating the same outcomes, over and over again?*

And finally, it dawned on me that, looking back, there were times in my life when I went all out. I didn't let anyone stop me. I had no distractions and, most importantly, failure was not an option. That's what happens when you have nothing to lose: you have a much, much higher risk tolerance. You figure there's nowhere to go but up, and you are very, very hungry to climb up from where you are. And you don't want to stay there a minute longer, so you hustle and hump and hurry to achieve your goals.

Reflecting on my past, that's the very attitude that marked my most significant levels of success. That "take no prisoners, I cannot fail, I will not fail, I want it all, I want it now" attitude was the rough outline of my greatest success stories.

So… what happened?

Where did that fire go?

How did I lose my hustle?

I also realized that once I had reached that level of excellence and started to reach some of my goals, acquire some possessions and show off the benchmarks of my success, I did what every successful person tells you never to do: I took my foot of the pedal and started to cost. I got comfortable, things got easier and, as a result, I started doing things that were the exact opposite of what got me there in the first place. It was like everything I had learned on the way up just got thrown out the window – or dribbled out my ear – once I hit that sweet spot.

I started becoming complacent. I forgot about my constant pursuit of becoming better and achieving more and sat back, enjoying the fruits of my hard labor. I started worrying about wanting more – more knowledge, more excellence, more success – and started worrying about protecting what I had.

Once I figured that out, once I saw what I had done, my life changed drastically. I started showing up every day wanting to make a significant change in my life from the day before. I wanted to feel like I accomplished something every day. I wanted to feel like I added value to some one's life. This became my mission.

I would out work, out play, outlive everyone I know. I would do it all with massive action. I would have urgency in my life so that I could enjoy everything, not only once I achieved each goal but while I was still achieving my steps to success.

The Takeaway

One thing successful people realize is that success never ends. If you want to stay on top, forget get to the top, you have to keep evolving, keep growing, keep achieving, keep bettering yourself. Comfort is the dream destroyer. You get comfy, you get lazy, you stop being hungry – even happy.

Most successful people absolutely enjoy the trappings of their success, but I honestly believe that more than the houses and the cars and the money and the fame, they enjoy what made them so successful in the first place.

Stephen King could have quite writing 40 books ago, and yet he still pumps them out, year after year. Why? Because he loves the thrill of what he does more than the comfort he's eared doing what he does.

Samuel L. Jackson was an extremely wealthy man before the Marvel films that introduced him to a whole new generation as "Nick Fury," so… why keep going? Why not just retire and count all his money every day? Like most successful people, artists in particular, passion fuels his success. How can you pass up the opportunity to work with so many great directors, producers, writers and fellow actors?

I could go on and on, but the one thing I'm trying to drive home in this chapter is how important it is to act on what you now know is your driving goal. However you envision your own Breakthrough, it will take All Out Massive Action to achieve it. But that's okay because, if you're still reading this, I'm more than confident that you're up for the task!

Action Steps for Chapter 8

Before you get started putting the lessons I've shared in Chapter 8, ask yourself these simple questions:

What does AOMA mean to you?

What does it look like?

How do you visualize it?

What actions are you currently taking to help you achieve your goals?

What could you accomplish by taking AOMA?

What would your Breakthrough look like if you took AOMA?

Chapter 9:
Master Your Mindset

Now that you've read, learned, lived and digested all 7 Strategies to Help You Unlock Your Greatest Potential, it's time to talk about the one vital tool that is going to tie them all together and maximize their power to help you Breakthrough.

Think about it for a minute: throughout this book, from chapter to chapter, everything we have talked about can all be boiled down to your mindset. From the time you wake up in the morning, get out of bed, brush your teeth, go down and kiss your spouse goodbye, get in the car and drive to work, you are living in a certain mindset.

How fast you move, what you do or forget to do, what you focus on, what you're preoccupied with, all has to do with the mindset you're in. Every single thought first started in your mind.

Control Your Thoughts, Control Your Destiny

So why is it so unbelievable that if you can start to control your thoughts and design what you're hearing on a day to day basis, that it could have a drastic impact on your life?

Let me explain it using this analogy: If you had a clear glass of water and all you did every day is add a teaspoon of dirt to it, over time that clear glass of water would become dark, murky and undesirable. Would you drink it? Probably not!

And yet that is what we do when we spend our lives surrounding ourselves with friends, peers, family members and colleagues who are constantly adding a little more dirt to our lives, one word, action or deed at a time. A little gossip here, a negative thought there, a doubtful concern here, a pessimistic thought there and, eventually, we start to take on the problems and the habits of the people that surround us.

We need to understand the power of our unspoken, unconscious mindset and learn how to limit the negativity around us so that our "glass of water" is clean, clear and unsullied. It's not okay to have those friends that are always negative; you know the ones I'm talking about. When they walk into a room the plants die. Who knows, this may even be you? (But not for long!)

I understand that some friends are hard to get rid of, and some "friends" are actually family members that you can't get rid of. But that doesn't mean you have to slavishly devote your time to them, at your own expense. I mentioned earlier the three types of friends we all have, but I feel like it's worth revisiting here: There are some of my friends that are three minute friends, folks that I know I can only be around them for three minutes. Anything more it will become toxic. They will suck me into their problems, constantly complaining about life and how it's everyone else's fault but their own.

Then I have my thirty minute friends where all we ever talk about is what's going on in their lives, how they're doing, what they're up to, how life is good – or bad – for them, but them never really asking about my life. They constantly interrupt to get their point across, the conversation is very one sided, but you listen because it's not about you, it's about being there for a friend.

And, lastly, there are my three hour friends. Now, I don't stay on the phone for three hours with anyone, but to serve this purpose of identifying a mutually beneficial conversation, this is the time title I give it!

This friend is very likeminded, you have equally good thoughts to contribute to the conversation, and there is a great amount of banter back and forth that excites both of you. You stimulate each other with great insight, observations and attention to details. You leave that conversation with a feeling of enjoyment and knowing that it was well worth your time. You see all of these types of friends play a role in your life.

Now, I revisit these three categories of friends because, depending on which one you spend the most time with, it will determine how clear or dirty your glass of water is. In other words, positive, energizing, inspiring friends will keep your water glass sparkling clean while those who always get you down, who are negative or selfish with your time will make your glass of water cloudy and dirty and undrinkable.

If you don't think who you hang around with is important, think again. I once heard a speaker say that your income and status will be directly influenced by the average of the top five people you hang around.

So if you hang around broke people, you will be broke. If you want to hang around lazy people, you will be lazy. If you hang around people who don't listen, you in turn will stop listening,. etc.

But if you want to be successful, get around successful people. If you want to improve yourself, hang around with folks who are always challenging to talk to, be around and hang out with. I always say if you're the smartest person in your group, it's time for a new group.

Success Isn't a Dollar Sign, It's a Mindset

It's not that successful people or rich people are better than you, they just think differently and they do things differently. Instead of paying all their bills first and invest what's left, they invest first and pay the bills with what's left. They understand that profits are king or queen. They constantly look for ways to improve, there are not satisfied with good. In fact, they can't stand good because they know that good is the enemy of great! So they strive to achieve greatness in all things they do.

It's not so much in their blood as it is in their mindset. Their mindset is always focused on the goal at hand, and once they achieve that goal, their brain immediately switches gears and time for the next one. Your thoughts play such a major part of your success that you ignore them at your own peril. And, quite frankly, I won't let you ignore them!

The Takeaway

You must condition your mind for greatness. The things you hear, the books you read, the people you hang around, will all shape you into your best you. It is the path that will finally help you have your Breakthrough!

Action Steps for Chapter 9

Before you start putting the lessons I've shared in Chapter 9 to work for you, ask yourself these simple questions:

Have I ever given serious thought to my mindset before?

Do I recognize the power of having a positive mindset?

Do I currently have a positive mindset?

Am I open to changing my current mindset?

How will I go about changing my mindset?

What is the first step I will take in creating a new mindset?

Chapter 10:
MORE

"Don't wish it were easier, wish you were better"
- Jim Rohn

No matter who you are, where you come from, or what you have, there is one thing that everyone needs. Right now some of you might even be wondering what it could possibly be that binds us all together. What do we all need? Simply put, we all need *more*.

Some of us may need more time. In fact, I'm pretty sure most of us need that in our lives. It seems like there are never enough hours in the day and I swear that New Year's comes faster every year. Some of us may need more money. More money can provide more security, offer us the opportunity to give to charity, or make providing for future generations easier. Most would agree that for any number of reasons more money would be a good thing. There is, however, one thing we all need more.

Freedom.

That's right, freedom. Take a moment and think about what exactly that means to you. What does more freedom in your life look like? What does it feel like? If you had more freedom what would you be doing on any given day? Go ahead and get a really good picture of it in your mind. Got it?

Now what would you say if I told you that it's possible to have that? What if I said it was possible to have all of it? What would you do with more time, more money, and more freedom? It's time to stop dreaming and make it happen.

Step 1 – Find

The first step to having more time, more money, and more freedom is to find out where you are, where you're going, and what stands in your way. Once you know these things you can start making a difference in your life.

Change is inevitable, either you control it or it controls you.

The first question you need to ask yourself is "Are you willing to make a change?" If you're not willing to make a change, willing to do something different to get more time, more money, and more freedom then there's no sense going any farther. The truth is that we can not achieve new and greater things without changing what we're currently doing. Let's face it, Albert Einstein sad it best. "The true definition of insanity is doing the same thing the same way and expecting a different result."

I know, change is hard. Believe me, I'm the first to admit it. Right about now you might be tempted to say that it's okay, you have enough in your life. Enough time, money and freedom. Let me ask you this, would you still have "enough" of all those things if your circumstances were changed by forces outside of your control? Let's face it, change is inevitable whether you're the one making it happen or not.

Would you still have enough time in your day, week, year, or life if an immediate family member was afflicted with a debilitating injury or illness? Would you have enough time if you were promoted to a job that required longer hours? Would you have enough time if you had a new baby or grandchild you needed to take care of or just wanted to spend time with? Probably not. That's not even talking about things like taking on a new hobby or more responsibility in your church or club or charitable group. Would you have enough time, If you were planning for retirement and saving money to build your nest egg? We all need more time now and we certainly need to plan for circumstances that will chew up the free time we think we have now.

So, what about money? Is "enough" actually good enough? If that family member was struck down by injury or illness would you be able to pay the hospital bills and not have to radically change your lifestyle to do it? What if you have an unexpected child or grandchild? Will your "enough" be able to handle the strain of paying for a college education in 18 years, maybe for two or three kids? What if an exciting new business opportunity comes your way? Would you be able to seize it without having to mortgage your house to do so? What if you wanted to walk away from the hustle and bustle of life and start spending quality time with your family? Could you do it? Could you afford to do it?

There's an old saying that when you have a problem you can either throw time or money at it. We tend to throw whichever we have the most of or value the least at those types of problems. Some problems even take both time and money to resolve. Do you have enough time or money to deal with those problems that come up without causing you additional problems or complications? Chances are you don't.

Even if you had all the time in the world, though, and enough money saved up not just for a rainy day but enough to get you through a flood of epic proportions, there's still one thing you need. You need more freedom. So, is your freedom worth making a few changes in your life? You better believe it is!

Honestly, where are you at?

So, if you've looked deep inside your heart and decided that it's time to make a change, the next step is to ask yourself where you're at right now. You need to know your starting point before you can properly map out a route to your destination. The good news is that in many ways this is the hardest thing you're going to do on your way to having more.

It's time to be honest with yourself. If you're not honest with yourself now it's going to cause you a whole lot of extra work and grief down the road. Lying to yourself at this point can't help you, but it will hurt you and make it hard for you to achieve the more that you deserve. Ignorance might be bliss today, but it will be a nightmare tomorrow.

So, write down a list of where you are now. Make sure to include areas like your finances, your relationships, your career, your health, your available time, and anything else that might be relevant.

The chains that bind you.

161

You've visualized what your *more* looks like. You've looked at where you are now and have committed to changing that, to have more. Now, before you get started on the road to more you have to figure out what's standing in your way. In other words, what's holding you back? Go ahead and write this down, too, remembering to be honest with yourself like before. It could be lack of education, shyness, a bad relationship, lack of support and encouragement, or any number of things. The truth is, whatever you believe in your heart is standing in the way of you achieving more in your life is a problem.

The mind is a powerful tool. What we believe, it can manifest in our lives. If we believe we are sick, we will probably spend more time being sick than others we know. If we believe we don't have enough education or experience then that self-doubt will be evident when we apply for jobs or ask for raises. If you don't have confidence in yourself how you can possibly expect others to? In any case, you need to identify and break these chains if you want to get from here to more.

Step 2 – Move

At this point you should have already imagined what more would look like to you. If you haven't, take a few minutes now and do so. Make sure to get a really good image in your head of more time, more money, more freedom and what you're doing with all of them. Maybe you haven't let yourself daydream or fantasize in a long while. Now is the time to do it! Give the vision as much detail as you can so that you can fix in your head exactly what it is you're doing the work for.

Take action!

Now that you have that image really fixed in your mind it's time to take steps to make that dream a reality. It's just like planning any journey. Think of it as a road trip, with stops on the way so you can rest, get gas for your car and food for yourself to help you make it all the way to your destination. The only way you're going to reach your destination, though, is if you know what route you're going to take to get there.

Think of your brain like a GPS system. By visualizing what you want out of life, what more time, money, and freedom looks like, you've input the coordinates of where you want to go into that GPS. By figuring out exactly where you are now, you gave the GPS your starting location. (This is why it's important to be honest with yourself in that step! Your brain's GPS is going to start at your house and map a route to your destination. You'll never get where you're going, though, if you can't give your GPS an accurate starting location.)

Now that you have your starting location and your destination both accurately inputted to your brain, it's time for it to do the work of mapping out the way to get from here to there. Remember, you don't have to take giant leaps to get where you're going. You just need steady progress. Small, baby steps are perfectly fine, and actually easier to accomplish both physically and mentally.

So, ask yourself, what is one thing you can do right at this minute to take a step toward that future you envision for yourself? Go on, think about it. What is one small thing you can do. Got it?

Great, now do it, right now! Don't worry, I'll wait for you to get back.

Play a mind game with yourself.

Congratulate yourself for taking that first step! And if you didn't take that first step, what are you reading this for? Okay, have you done it? Yes? Then we can move on.

When you start any new endeavor one of the biggest obstacles to overcome is yourself. Old habits, old beliefs, and old ways of thinking will just get in your way. The best way to conquer these is to instill new habits that help change the way you do things and view yourself.

Make a commitment to yourself to do one thing a day, no matter how small, to keep progressing on your path. Ideally pick a time of day where you can spend time focusing on taking those steps and schedule it into your routine. Then any time you get tired or bored or lazy remind yourself of the vision of having more and let that drive you to take that next step even if you didn't feel like it ten minutes earlier. Just keep taking those steps and eventually you'll get there.

Step 3 – Adjust

Have you ever been driving in your car, heading someplace you've never been, when your GPS suddenly tells you that it's recalculating your route? Maybe you missed your exit, or didn't turn on the right street, or had an obstacle like a roadblock or accident thrown into your path. Or, perhaps you reached your destination and then decided you wanted to travel on to the next town over.

Your GPS is now tasked with calculating how to get from your new location to the next.

It's the same with your mind and the goals you set for yourself. Sometimes you'll find that the steps you set out for yourself aren't working or are taking you on a detour away from where you want to go or a roadblock you can't surmount gets put up in front of you. That's the time to adjust your plan and change your steps enough to get back on course toward your destination.

When you finally do reach your destination it's time to take stock. This destination is your new home. Are you happy with it? Do you have everything you need? Or is there more that you can see now that is just outside your grasp, but with a little work could be yours? It might be time to start the next phase of your journey, repeating the steps you took to get this far.

Make it bigger

No matter what you achieve, now is the time to finesse it. It's time to create a new dream and set out on the path to it. If you wanted to sell a million dollars worth of merchandise now it's time to try for ten million. If you achieved writing a book it's time to look at the next ten books you're going to write. Take your achievement and increase it by a magnitude of ten or, as Grant Cardone likes to say, 10x your results. If you did that how much more time, money, and freedom would you have then?

As long as you are breathing you should be striving to have a better life than the one you have today. You deserve an abundant life. You deserve a secure future for you and your entire family. You deserve more.

The Takeaway

The world is constantly pushing toward a state of decay. This is called entropy. To overcome it we need to keep moving, keep forging forward. As long as we draw breath there are things we can be doing, lives we can be touching, ways in which we can have more abundance and freedom.

In order to have more time, money, and freedom you must first visualize what you want and then make a plan to make it happen. Don't be afraid to correct course along the way. When you get to your destination, remember, it's not your final one. Not yet. The plan is to keep taking baby steps toward being your best and having the freedom to do what you love.

Action Steps for Chapter 10

Ask yourself these questions as you get ready to implement the steps in this chapter.

What does it mean to me to have more?

What would I do with more time?

What would I do with more money?

What would I do with more freedom?

Do I have a dream?

What does that dream look like?

Where am I now in relation to that dream?

What is standing in my way?

Which step can I take right away to give myself some momentum and a feeling of accomplishment?

How many steps do I think it's going to take to achieve the more that I'm looking for?

Am I ready to make a change?

What am I waiting for?

Need help with all of these steps? Sign up now for my nine-week coaching course that will step you through the process to make more time, more money, and more freedom all within your grasp. Just visit www.corychapman.com to sign up and get more information. I'll see you there and together we'll strive for MORE.

Epilogue:
Putting it All Together

So, there you have it: 7 Strategies to Help You Unlock Your Greatest Potential. Each one of these strategies is a journey unto itself, and a positive step in the right direction. Each one is linked to the next, and together they create an environment that is ripe for growth, opportunity and becoming your very, ultimately, limitless best.

Gentle Reminders for Breakthrough Success!

I hope you've enjoyed our time together and that you're already well underway on your journey to Breakthrough. Or, at the very least, ready to start the process anew. Here are just few things to keep in mind before we part:

- **There is no timeline:** Timing is everything and growth is internal. We talk a lot about speed toward the end of this book, but what is fast for me might be slow for you, and vice versa. Proceed at your own pace, trust your gut and follow your own internal timeline for success.
- **Continue to "edit" your story:** Never forget the power of the story you tell yourself, all day, each and every day. Words are so incredibly powerful, and yet we take them for granted far too often. Every time your story turns dark, anxious or negative, stop right there, focus and rewrite it continually. Only by

169

constant perseverance and diligence can you habitually change your story from the dark to the light, from the negative to the positive.

- **Focus on your why:** Human nature is such that inspiration becomes temporary, which is why our "why" is so important. Remember your why, and use it to continually tell yourself a positive, nurturing and helpful story instead of the negative, harmful one you've been living for years.
- **Know yourself; be yourself:** No one can do this for you; you have to take the steps yourself. Trust yourself to take the right ones or make strong, firm and confident decisions if you misstep. Take counsel from others, mastermind frequently but always stay true to your own compass and chart your own path.
- **Always be evolving:** Finally, no matter how soon your Breakthrough comes, or how big it might be, congratulate yourself, enjoy a little bubbly and then, the very next day… keep moving forward. Never stop to rest and flatter yourself and grow cozy in your new position. Learn a little every day and that little turns into a lot.

All that being said, though, it's time to take what you've learned and apply it to your own journey. Advice is fine, but action is necessary to turn your dreams into reality. And speaking of action…

The End of the Story: *Or A New Beginning?*

Back at the beginning of this book I told you about the trials and tribulations that I had gone through, but what

I didn't get a chance to tell you is how the story unfolded. After 2008, I rebuilt once again and started EFC Wealth Group, Inc., but this time with just me and my wife. We had very loyal clients who stuck with us for better or worse.

We continued to build and, along the way, gather millions of dollars in assets under management. The business started to thrive and, instead of diversifying in sectors like I did before, we diversified in industries. We started new business in the direct sales industry, which taught us how to lead people and develop networks.

I also became a speaker and author in the personal development arena. After all, through the journey of my life experience I have become an expert on what *not* to do! Who knew there was a market out there that would pay to avoid the same mistakes I've made? More importantly, I could make a great life for my family and I while helping other people change their circumstances through strategies that I have learned and experienced firsthand.

I started my own success coaching business and started speaking on stages to thousands of people, teaching them about Wealth, Business, Relationships and Health. This story is evolving into my "future life," as I explained in my book.

I want to thank you for buying this book. I hope that my experiences and strategies can help you achieve whatever you desire out of life. Whether it's reconnecting with someone, starting a new career or building your own business, when put together these simple strategies will catapult you in the right direction to success.

I wish you well along the way and hope that you won't be too shy to let me know how you're doing. I can be reached at cory@thebookbreakthrough.com and would love to hear more about how you're achieving – or have achieved – your Breakthrough. Who knows, we may even mastermind some day!

Also, feel free to visit me at any of the following locations:

- **Website:** http://corychapman.com
- **YouTube:** https://www.youtube.com/user/corychapmanintl/
- **Twitter:** https://twitter.com/coryjchapman
- **Google+:** https://plus.google.com/u/0/+CoryChapmanintl/posts
- **Facebook:** /corychapman.com

I'd love to hear from you!!!

Action Steps for the Epilogue

Before you get started using the lessons I've shared in the Epilogue, ask yourself these simple questions:

What is my next step for moving forward?

What am I excited about doing first?

What is the first goal I want to achieve?

How am I going to achieve it?

Does my Breakthrough look any clearer now?

Who can I share this information with?

Who will benefit from it the most?

How soon can I get it to them?

www.ingramcontent.com/pod-product-compliance
Lightning Source LLC
Chambersburg PA
CBHW022056210326
41519CB00054B/528